CONNECTING WITH MAX

CONNECTING WITH MAX

HOW MEDICATION CLOSED THE GAP
BETWEEN A FAMILY AND THEIR SON WITH AUTISM

THE ORP LIBRARY

WRITTEN BY
JEFF KRUKAR, PH.D.
KATIE GUTIERREZ
CHELSEA McCUTCHIN
WITH
NICOLETTE WEISENSEL, M.D.
JAMES G. BALESTRIERI

WRITERS OF THE ROUND TABLE PRESS
PO BOX 511
HIGHLAND PARK, IL 60035

Publisher	COREY MICHAEL BLAKE
Executive Editor	KATIE GUTIERREZ
Lead Writer	CHELSEA MCCUTCHIN
President	KRISTIN WESTBERG
Facts Keeper	MIKE WINICOUR
Cover Design	ANALEE PAZ
Interior Design and Layout	SUNNY DIMARTINO
Proofreading	JONATHAN HIERHOLZER
Last Looks	CHRISTIAN PANNECK
Digital Book Conversion	SUNNY DIMARTINO
Digital Publishing	SUNNY DIMARTINO

Printed in the United States of America
First Edition: March 2016
10 9 8 7 6 5 4 3 2 1

Library of Congress Cataloging-in-Publication Data
Krukar, Jeff
Connecting with max: how medication closed the gap
between a family and their son with autism /
Jeff Krukar, Katie Gutierrez, and Chelsea McCutchin
with Nicolette Weisensel and James G. Balestrieri.—1st ed. p. cm.
Print ISBN: 978-1-939418-79-1   Digital ISBN: 978-1-939418-80-7
Library of Congress Control Number: 2016933038
Number 14 in the series: The ORP Library
The ORP Library: Connecting with Max

RTC Publishing is an imprint of Writers of the Round Table, Inc.
Writers of the Round Table Press and the RTC Publishing logo
are trademarks of Writers of the Round Table, Inc.

CONTENTS

INTRODUCTION

Today, according to the U.S. Department of Health and Human Services, more than 5.5 million children—or eight percent of kids—in the U.S. have some form of disability. Whether the problem is physical, behavioral, or emotional, these children struggle to communicate, learn, and relate to others. While there is no longer *segregation* in the same sense as there was in the 1950s, what remains the same is the struggle. Even with all of our resources and technology, parents of children with disabilities fight battles every day to find the help and education their children need.

I have led Oconomowoc Residential Programs (ORP) for over thirty years. We're a family of companies offering specialized services and care for children, adolescents, and adults with disabilities. Too often, when parents of children with disabilities try to find funding for programs like ours, they are bombarded by red tape, conflicting information, or no information at all, so they struggle blindly for years to secure an appropriate education. Meanwhile, home life, and the child's wellbeing, suffers. In cases when parents and caretakers have exhausted their options—and their hope—ORP is here to help. We felt it was time to offer parents a new, unexpected tool to fight back: stories that educate, empower, and inspire.

The original idea was to create a library of comic books that could empower families with information to reclaim their rights. We wanted to give parents and caretakers the information they need to advocate for themselves, as well as provide educators and therapists with a therapeutic tool. And, of course, we wanted to reach the children—to offer them a visual representation of their journey that would show that they aren't alone, nor are they wrong or "bad" for their differences. What we found in the process of writing original stories for the comics is that these journeys are too long, too complex, to be contained within a standard comic. So what we are now creating is an ORP library of disabilities books—traditional books geared toward parents, caretakers, educators, and therapists, *and* comic books portraying the world through the eyes of children with disabilities. Both styles of books share what we have learned while advocating for families over the years while also honestly highlighting their emotional journeys. We're creating communication devices that anyone can read to understand complex disabilities in a new way.

In an ideal situation, these books will be used therapeutically, to communicate the message, and to help support the work ORP and companies like ours are doing. The industry has changed dramatically and is not likely to turn around any time soon—certainly not without more people being aware of families' struggles. We have an opportunity to put a face to the conversation, reach out to families, and start that dialogue.

Caring for children with disabilities consumes your life. We know that. And we want you to realize, through these stories, that you are not alone. We can help.

Sincerely,
Jim Balestrieri
CEO, Oconomowoc Residential Programs
www.orplibrary.com

A NOTE ABOUT THIS BOOK

Psychotropic medications are prescribed for the treatment of psychiatric disorders and specifically to improve a patient's emotional and behavioral health. In children and adolescents, just as in adults, lack of appropriate treatment can result in both short-term and long-term consequences.

Since the mid to late 1990s, there has been a significant increase in the understanding of childhood psychiatric disorders and a developing evidence base to support psychotropic medication and other nonmedication treatments for children with these disorders. Unfortunately, despite these advances, the majority of children and adolescents do not receive appropriate evaluations and treatment.

Changes in the U.S. mental health system over the last 20 years have resulted in a shortage of child and adolescent psychiatrists, increasingly limited insurance coverage for inpatient and residential treatment, and limited outpatient alternatives to support what many believe is an increased need for services. The front lines of the mental health services battle now squarely reside in the office of the primary care provider. These physicians now furnish over half of the mental health treatment in the U.S. and are believed to prescribe the majority of psychotropic medications used by children and adolescents (Bazelton Center). While each primary care provider's education and experience varies, most are unlikely to have the appropriate resources to treat youth who have a complicated set of challenges.

Unfortunately, there has also been an insufficient number of psychotropic medication trials with children and adolescents. This has left few psychotropic medications that are Food and Drug Administration (FDA) approved for use in youth. As a result, many psychotropic medications prescribed for this age group are administered "off label"—that is, not FDA approved for use in children and adolescents for certain disorders or age ranges. In clinical practice, however, the majority of "off label" psychotropic medications do appear to be beneficial and safe in youth.

Psychotropic medications are only one component of a comprehensive biopsychosocial treatment plan, which must be a collaborative team effort and include other components in addition to medication. The term *biopsychosocial* recognizes the three domains that impact a youth's emotional and behavioral well-being:

1. *Bio* refers to "biological," and includes physical health and genetic factors. Psychotropic medications affect biological factors by altering the levels of chemicals in the brain that help to regulate the activity of neurons (brain cells) that determine emotions, mood, and behavior.

2. *Psycho* refers to psychological factors in the youth that contribute to emotional and behavioral functioning, including feelings and thoughts, goals, and understanding of self and environment.

3. *Social* refers to the environmental factors that influence a youth's functioning, such as family circumstances and relationships and other resources in the community, including those provided by human service agencies and natural supports. Within the social domain, it is particularly important to obtain the evaluation of history of trauma and disrupted attachments.

Health professionals, families, advocates, and human service providers must carefully assess the risks and benefits of using psychotropic medications in children and adolescents. Readers are encouraged to educate themselves appropriately depending on their individual situation, and to be careful to obtain information from reputable sources. An appendix is located at the end of this book with resources to consider using.

The young man depicted in the following story struggles with significant emotional and behavioral difficulties. You may note similarities to your own experiences or those of a loved one, student, or patient. If so, this book is meant to provide a roadmap, of sorts. It is our hope that the education it provides will help you navigate the complex journey experienced by those whose worlds intersect with the use of psychotropic medications.

Jim Balestrieri
CEO, Oconomowoc Residential Programs

CHAPTER 1

Aaron reached over to rest his hand on his wife's knee. Diana was fiddling with her wedding band, pulling it up to the knob of her knuckle, twisting, then lowering it again. Her shoulders were rigid, hiked up so that her neck looked shortened and tight. She'd complain later, rolling her neck around, saying she must have slept wrong. She was rarely aware of the physicality of her nervousness. Then again, maybe that was everyone.

At his touch, Diana glanced at him and gave a rueful smile. "Is it that obvious?"

"Only to someone who's feeling the same," Aaron said.

He, too, felt coiled with tension about seeing Max for the first time in a month. He hadn't been able to shake the guilt at having placed his son into residential treatment. Max had been diagnosed with PDD-NOS—pervasive developmental disorder not otherwise speci-fied—when he was four. Recently, that diagnosis was changed to autism spectrum disorder. It was just a name change—a label, Aaron thought, that was probably easier for doctors to use for insurance purposes—but it had devastated them. PDD-NOS sounded vague enough to suggest there was a solution they simply hadn't discov-ered, or perhaps that it would somehow resolve itself, once Max got older. Autism spectrum disorder carried a different weight, one their family had been unable to set down in the two years since the re-diagnosis.

> PDD-NOS is a diagnosis given to individuals with severe and pervasive impairment in the development of reciprocal social interaction associated with either verbal or nonverbal communication skills or with the presence of stereotyped behavior, interests, and activities. Historically, this diagnosis was used when individuals did not meet diagnostic criteria for another pervasive developmental disorder such as autistic disorder. Beginning in 2013 (DSM-5), this diagnosis is no longer used and instead a diagnosis of autism spectrum disorder is used.

Max required substantial care and support at home, at school, and in the community. While he could often communicate verbally in short phrases, his inflexible thinking and inability to read social cues and interactions set him far apart from his peers. He could also become aggressive and frighteningly self-injurious. He was just frustrated, Aaron knew, at being unable to express his emotions, his experience of the world around him. How would you feel, he'd tried explaining to friends and family over the years, if you lacked the language and self-awareness to tell someone there was way too much noise and you needed to leave the room or take a break? How would you feel in a meeting if everyone talked over you, ignoring your attempts to get their attention? How would you feel if you were afraid but did not know how to ask for comfort? Aaron thought of Max's frustration as comparable to infants screaming—as ear-piercing as those howls were, babies didn't cry to provoke their parents. They cried to communicate, in the only way available to them.

Self-injurious behavior (SIB) in ASD is often seen and related to sensory-seeking needs or dysregulation. SIB is different than suicidal behavior, which is behavior done with the goal of ending one's life.

But when Max had recently turned on Diana in a rage, they'd all discovered that, at twelve, he finally overpowered her in strength. Aaron had been out of town at a yoga retreat, and Diana, in desperation, called the police. Although Diana had refused the seventy-two-hour psychiatric care stay for Max that was recommended by the hospital, Aaron had heard about The Springs, a residential care setting that served as a retreat more than a hospital for those on the autism spectrum. While Max had qualified for waiver services, they were still on the wait list for the Children's Long Term Support (CLTS) waiver to receive any type of support in their home. In the meantime, a residential placement was their best option.

Medicaid waiver services are vehicles states can use to test new or existing ways to deliver and pay for health care services in Medicaid and the Children's Health Insurance Program, or CHIP.

Aaron relied on natural remedies as much as he could, and he was thrilled that his son's monthlong stay at The Springs would include a gluten- and casein-free diet, as well as green juicing and a special blend of patented, all-natural supplements that he would receive by injection weekly, including additional nutrients to help his body detoxify; studies indicated that children with autism often weren't capable of detoxifying their own bodies, and mercury poisoning as well as zinc deficiencies could contribute to the worsening of symptoms. The Springs also offered daily acupressure, yoga, and meditation techniques that were specially designed to help children with ASD. In all, The Springs seemed a far cry from the kind of residential treatment center Aaron had always envisioned existing for children like Max. Diana, who had been exhausted and distraught, with a black eye and two terrified younger sons, had told Aaron to make the call. It was a strange, contradictory feeling: a sense of shame in leaving his son in the care of strangers, mixed with a sense of male pride at protecting and serving the rest of his family.

> *Biomedical treatment* is a term that includes a variety of treatments not approved by the FDA for treatment of autistic spectrum disorders, including specialized diets, gut treatments, immune regulation, vitamins, and other supplements. There are a number of controversial therapies or interventions available, but few, if any, are supported by scientific studies. Parents should use caution before adopting any unproven treatments. Although dietary interventions have been helpful in some children, parents should be careful to closely monitor their child's nutritional status.

Now, they pulled up to The Springs and parked their Volvo station wagon in the makeshift lot. Aaron took Diana's hand as they walked into the main building, where they'd left Max four weeks earlier. The sadness in his eyes needed no words to translate.

Today, Max was sitting beside a direct care worker with a sketchbook in his lap. His dark hair had grown, covering the tops of his ears. To Aaron's eyes, he also looked about an inch taller, and his skin was flushed and healthy.

"Beautiful boy!" Diana exclaimed as she walked over to her son. She'd sung the John Lennon song to him since he was born, and Max was accustomed to the nickname,

4

though he didn't understand its origin. He gave his mother a small forced smile before looking back down at his sketchbook. Then, as if remembering that he should stand to hug her, he made his way to his feet. He let Diana and Aaron wrap their arms around him. Though he didn't return the embrace, he didn't pull away the way he did so often. That was a positive sign.

The direct care worker, a college-aged woman with blond hair pulled into a low bun, smiled at the family. She asked how their drive had been and then said that Mr. Perth, the senior interventionist, was waiting to speak with them. "I'll take you over when you're ready," she said.

Diana nodded. "Why don't you get your things," she said to Max, "and then we'll go talk with Mr. Perth." She was careful not to overwhelm him with too many instructional steps; he responded best with a "first, then" ordering.

Without speaking, Max slipped his backpack over his shoulders and held his sketchbook to his chest. He trailed behind his parents to the administrator's office, where Mr. Perth, the program coordinator, was waiting to speak to them.

"Hello, it's so good to see you both again." Mr. Perth stood, extending his hand for Aaron and Diana to shake.

"It's nice to see you again, too," Aaron said, shaking the man's hand. Mr. Perth had served as Aaron and Diana's primary contact through Max's program, calling or sending daily emails describing Max's progress. He was a portly British man who smelled like spearmint gum and hair wax.

"This is our dismissal program, which will be brief."

Mr. Perth handed over a folder stuffed thick with paperwork. "This is Max's paperwork, and inside I've also included the information on continuing his injectable supplements. You can bring him back here or, since you live quite a distance away, we have a mail order program where you can order a week's supply at a time. They're shipped overnight to maintain their temperature and integrity. I've already included a week's supply for you to take home today for Max's continued treatment regime."

Aaron flipped open the packet and had to stop himself from gasping at the cost of the continued supplements, as well the outrageous number of pills his kid would have to take each day! Four pills of Primer in the morning, followed by vitamin D3 drops at breakfast. Primal defense supplement just before lunch and molybdenum just after. Zinc sulfate cream after every bath or shower, primrose oil on acupressure points, and Diflucan to continue treating his overactive yeast in the gut. The injectable just before bed. Insurance hadn't covered the cost of alternative treatment, and between residential care and the cost of supplements, the month Max had spent at The Springs had made a considerable dent on the family's savings.

"Additionally, you'll find a list of the supplements that we used daily. We have preferred brands, but you could pick them up at a local drugstore, if you're not as concerned with quality," Mr. Perth said, which Aaron found rather snooty.

"Thank you, Mr. Perth." Aaron forced a smile and slid the folder under his arm.

"Well, I'm sure you'll want to get home before it gets too late. You have quite the drive ahead of you." Mr. Perth stood, and Aaron reminded himself to keep calm. Though he felt rushed now, he supposed that Mr. Perth had kept in frequent enough communication throughout the month that there probably weren't many details he and Diana didn't know about their son's stay. Besides, Aaron just wanted to get Max home, to spend time with him and see for himself what kinds of improvement the supplements and nutrition had made on his behaviors. He was hoping they had made him less anxious, less likely to have such intense meltdowns. Aaron was prepared to follow through with the program as closely as possible at home if it was working, but—aside from not pulling away from their hug—he wasn't overly impressed by Max's demeanor so far.

After loading Max's bag into the trunk of the Volvo, Aaron slid back behind the driver's seat and headed toward the highway.

"We're happy to see you, Max," he called into the backseat, glancing at his son in the rearview mirror. He was so handsome, with his thick, dark hair, serious long-lashed eyes, and smattering of freckles. In another life, the girls wouldn't have left him alone. Aaron swallowed past the grief that was always present for the life Max wouldn't live. He asked, "What would you like for dinner?"

"Pizza," Max said instantly.

"Well, we can't have any gluten or dairy, bud. But we could try—"

"Pizza!" Max shouted. "Pizza!" He pressed forward against the seatbelt, throwing a closed fist against the back of Aaron's chair with each fervent cry of "Pizza!"

Aaron's stomach sank as he and Diana exchanged glances. Max struggled with being told no, making transitions, and changing routines. The day of his last rage, his normal bus driver was sick and the substitute driver had been late to pick him up. That small change was enough to light a fuse that had taken hours to tamp, ending in bruises and heartache. If this was Max's behavior five minutes into their drive, what did it indicate about the progress—or lack thereof—he'd made in the last month?

"Let me see if I can find a place that will do a gluten- and cheese-free pizza," Diana said quietly. "Max, would you like that? It's a compromise. You get pizza, and we make sure you're eating foods that are good for you."

"I! Don't! Care! I want pizza!" Max shouted from the backseat.

Aaron took a deep breath. Max seemed just the same as a month ago.

• • •

It had been strange when Max was gone. Diana had felt in a haze the first few days, sinking into and out of deep, sticky sleep. Aaron had told her there was such a thing as sleep debt, and her body was trying to "repay" the sleep it had lost in recent months. Diana had given a wan smile, telling Aaron she hadn't slept in *years*, not months, and that if sleep had a debt collector—a sleep bookie—her kneecaps would be broken by now. But he was right: after the first week, her schedule became more normal, less single-mindedly driven toward bed. Thank goodness for Aaron, she thought, swooping into full dad-mode while she caught up on rest. She wasn't sure what she'd do without him—raising three boys, one on the spectrum, alone? The thought was unbearable, and she ached for those mothers in that position.

As the weeks had passed with Max at The Springs,

Diana couldn't help noticing small but significant changes in their household. Justin and Aiden yelled while they played video games, for example, emitting the joyful, raucous sounds of boyhood that had been absent in their home because loud noises set Max off. Diana stood just outside the living room, watching them. They were carefree, she thought, their bony elbows and shoulders jerking every which way as they manipulated animated soldiers. She wondered how much they had to restrain themselves on a daily basis and felt a moment of anger— not toward Max but toward the general unfairness of one child trapped inside his mind and another two forced into miniature adulthood. She was glad the boys had a reprieve, even if it was brief.

And she and Aaron had actually managed to have sex—not just once, but twice! Before this, Diana wasn't sure when she'd last felt the weight of his lean, strong body on hers. Had it been two months? Three? They were on different schedules most of the time, with one falling asleep before the other, and even when they were awake in bed at the same time, Diana was so bleary with exhaustion and—yes, some days, despair—that sex was the last thing on her mind. There were nights Aaron would touch her ribcage lightly, questioningly, and she would pat his hand and roll just slightly farther away. With a pang, she sometimes thought back to their early days of marriage, before the boys—before Max—when Aaron's body was as familiar to her, and more beloved, than her own. Now, she'd been surprised by the feel of him, by the sense that they were two such separate people. She'd wanted the lights off, the better to conceal the softness of her belly and wideness of her thighs. But there was no denying it: the intimacy felt wonderful. They'd held hands afterwards, and Aaron had said, still out of breath, "Let's never go that long again." She'd nodded, but she knew—as soon as Max was home, their real lives would return.

And she *wanted* Max home. That was the thing. Without him, she felt constantly as if she were forgetting something essential, as though she'd walked out of the house without pants or even legs. He was her firstborn; she'd carried him inside her the way she still carried him inside her. As challenging as his disorder made their lives, she would never trade it for life without him. She *needed* him home . . . yet she dreaded it. There was no such thing as uncomplicated love for a child with autism.

Before Aaron and Diana had picked up Max, they had sat down with Justin and Aiden and discussed the changes they would be making as a household in order to continue the care and treatment Max had received at The Springs. The boys were disappointed about the new dietary restrictions for family meals, but the biggest concern that neither could fully express was the fear that Max's temper hadn't subsided. He was a head taller than the two of them, and while he never *meant* to scare or hurt anyone, those things happened anyway.

The day after they brought him home, Aaron and Diana planned a family outing.

Diana had organized a family picnic, followed by kicking the soccer ball around in Max's favorite park. When Max was younger, he could spend hours there on the swing. The rhythmic motion seemed to soothe him, to regulate him in some way. She hoped he got some of the same comfort and pleasure out of being at the park today.

As Diana distributed foil-wrapped roast beef sandwiches on gluten-free bread, she smiled at her sons. Sitting in a row, their physical resemblance was striking. They were tall and lean like their father, with the same dark hair and olive skin, and they'd each inherited Diana's father's eyes, the color she'd imagined the ocean to be before she ever saw it. She took her seat with Aaron across the picnic table and watched them each carefully unwrap their sandwiches. It had been so long since they were all together that she relished even the sounds of foil crinkling against the wood of the picnic table. She gave them each a bottle of water and then reached over to hand Max his supplements.

"No! No pills!" Max said, slapping Diana's hand so the vitamins scattered onto the dirt at his feet.

"Max," Diana said, keeping her voice calm. "It's time for your vitamins."

"No more pills!" Max said, starting to rock forward on the bench seat.

"Come on, dude," Aaron said. "Now you're going to miss your vitamins for lunch. We don't have any more here." He tried to keep his voice level, even a little playful, but his body stiffened. He knew this defiant attitude, and he hated it—not only because of how disruptive it was and how Max must be feeling underneath it, but because of how Justin and Aiden must perceive it. They loved their brother, but Aaron also knew they didn't understand him. They saw him as loud and weird and sometimes scary. They used to complain about how he got all the attention, but now they accepted it with quiet resignation. Aaron often worried about the effect that Max's behavior—particularly these outbursts—would have on them long-term. How would they view their brother as adults? How would they think back on their childhoods?

"No!" Max banged his hand on the picnic table so hard that when he drew it up to repeat the action, nine-year-old Justin yelled, "Mom! Max is bleeding!"

Max didn't react well to sudden loud noises, especially those from people. He covered his ears and screamed with all of the power in his lungs. Justin's eyes opened wide and filled with tears. He was the most sensitive of the boys. Living without Max for a month had made him forget some of his brother's nuances, and Aaron could see Justin mentally berating himself for yelling when Max wasn't expecting it.

Aaron rose and swiftly crossed the table. From behind, he held Max by the shoulders and gave him some deep pressure. "Come on, Max. Not now. Let's take a deep breath."

Max reached up and grabbed his father's forearms, throwing his head back into his dad's sternum so that Aaron stumbled and they both fell to the ground, grunting with the unexpected impact on tree roots and stones. Aaron wrapped his arms around Max again and embraced his son close to his chest from behind, holding him tightly until Max was able to calm and regain self-control. After a few minutes, everything quieted except the sniffling and soft, muffled sobs coming from Justin, who'd buried his face in Diana's chest. Aaron felt Max's struggle calm into a random twitch every now and then, and he stared up into the trees. Two male cardinals watched quizzically from a branch, then flew away. Tomorrow, Max would go back to school. Aaron had sold a solid bill of goods to Max's teachers about his improvement, but now, a sense of dread washed over him.

Time had passed, but nothing had changed.

•••

Two weeks after Max returned home, Diana dropped the boys off at school and came home to her empty, quiet house. She'd been a homemaker from the time Max was born, but while he was in residential treatment, she'd decided to take on a part-time job at her good friend's nonprofit. She was only writing press releases and helping schedule events, but she was pleased that she was finally putting her bachelor's degree in mass communications to some use. She needed to be at the office at eleven a.m., and since the boys needed to be dropped off at school at eight-thirty, she had plenty of time to get ready.

She'd just emerged from the shower and was putting a pod into her coffeemaker when she noticed she had voicemail from Max's school. No, no, no, she thought, closing her eyes. For a second, she considered pretending that she hadn't seen it. She'd make her coffee, get dressed, and head into work, spending a few blissful hours thinking about other things—the world beyond her home and family—before picking the boys up from school. She exhaled. No. She couldn't do that. Without bothering to make her coffee, she played the message: Max's teacher was asking that she come get him as soon as possible. Mentally, Diana bade farewell to the day she'd envisioned.

At the principal's office, Max was rocking back and forth on a bench, covering his forehead with an icepack.

"Beautiful boy!" Diana exclaimed. "What happened to you?"

Mrs. Deveraux, the principal, came out of her office when she saw Diana's red hair through her office window. "Diana. I'm so glad you came."

"Of course. I'm sorry I didn't call back. I just wanted to get here as soon as I could. What happened?" Diana looked down at her son, who hadn't even acknowledged her.

"No one has been able to get him to move since the school nurse got him to that bench," Mrs. Deveraux said. "Perhaps it would be better if he stayed out here while we chat." Reluctantly, Diana followed the principal into her office, where she left the door open to keep an eye on her son.

"Max has had an interesting time back at school," Mrs. Deveraux said carefully. "We've been dealing with his inattentiveness and frequent frustration and agitation in the classroom, and it hasn't been unmanageable. But today we hit a fever pitch. He didn't want to switch tasks, and when his teacher asked him again, he stood up and shoved his desk at her. Thankfully, she was too far away for it to hurt her. But then Max went to the cement wall and started banging his head against it. His teacher couldn't pull him away—she thought he was going to give himself a concussion! Diana, we've had Max here for six years, and while we've seen mild self-injurious behavior from him before, we've never seen this intensity and severity."

Diana winced at the thought of her son causing himself such pain. Max had exhibited self-injurious behavior when he was very young, and it had been terrifying: he'd throw his head onto the table, against the wall, once even breaking a window—but it had decreased significantly as he got older. The occupational therapy had helped him learn to self-regulate more effectively.

Sensory regulation strategies can be used as part of a comprehensive treatment of autism spectrum disorders since individuals with these disorders often can have difficulties with sensory integration not developing properly. Sounds, sights, and movement may seem more chaotic, more distracting, and stronger than they do to others. Balance and coordination may also be a problem. Because of these sensory problems, a child may avoid the playful, sensory-rich experiences that are natural building blocks to learning and developing relationships.

An *occupational therapist* (O.T.) is a master's degree–trained individual who treats injured, ill, or disabled patients through the therapeutic use of everyday activities. They help these patients develop, recover, and improve the skills needed for daily living and working. O.T.s who are trained in sensory techniques will engage a child in playful activities designed to help him process the information he receives from his senses in a more typical manner.

"I know that Max was in a therapeutic residential setting for a month," Mrs. Deveraux continued. "Perhaps that, coupled with an uneasy transition back home, has contributed to what we're seeing now?"

Diana nodded. That made sense. Of course, there were always so many possibilities for what Max was thinking and feeling and trying like hell to express, and she never knew which was accurate. Early on, when Justin and Aiden were tiny and needed her attention constantly, Aaron had taken the lead in Max's autism care. Back then, she had sent up prayers of thanks for her husband. She knew how fortunate she was that he was so involved. But lately, and especially seeing Max's lack of improvement since The Springs, she wasn't sure whether they were doing enough. Somehow, it was as if she'd forfeited a voice in Max's treatment plan, and she wasn't sure how to speak up.

"I'll take him home. Aaron and I will talk everything over tonight," Diana finally mustered.

She got Max into the backseat of her car, and as she buckled her own seatbelt, her throat was tight with emotion. The only real improvement Max had made from the time he was diagnosed at four was in his speech. They'd gone the all-natural route—no medications of any kind—Aaron had insisted upon for the past eight years. But now she wasn't sure whom that was serving—Max or her husband. She remembered hearing once that health existed on a spiral: it was always either climbing upwards, improving bit by bit, or falling downwards, to eventual catastrophe—no staying still. All signs pointed to Max sliding down. The definition of insanity . . . Diana thought as she drove the familiar route home. It was time to try something different.

> A *speech therapist* (also known as a speech-language pathologist) is a master's degree–trained individual who assesses, diagnoses, treats, and helps to prevent communication and swallowing disorders. Speech, language, and swallowing disorders result from a variety of causes, including ASD.

CHAPTER 2

Aaron crossed his legs before shifting and crossing them the other way. He was completely out of his comfort zone in the pediatrician's office. All three of their sons had seen the same doctor since they were born, but Dr. Peterson had recently retired and another physician had taken over the practice. Not only was Aaron entering unknown territory by seeking a conventional Western approach to his son's challenges, he was also trying it with a doctor who wasn't intimately acquainted with Max. Diana put her hand on Aaron's back, rubbing gently between his shoulder blades.

When Aaron had come home from work the night before, Diana had told him about what had happened at school. She told him she was afraid for Max and admitted that she was frustrated, that she wondered whether they could and should be doing more for him. Her eyes were wide and beseeching, begging him to support her, but they also held a sense of determination. Indeed, she'd already scheduled an appointment with the new pediatrician for the following morning. Without waiting for him to react, she'd asked that he come with her, that he keep an open mind, and he'd agreed, with the caveat that they continue Max's gluten- and casein-free diet and the vitamin supplements, if not the nutritional ones. She nodded, and the next morning they found themselves sitting in the pediatrician's office, where framed teddy bear posters were juxtaposed with cold white tile and the smell of disinfectant.

Max sat on the exam table with his iPad, oblivious to his parents' interactions. He'd found a new app that he loved, and as long as he could play his country music through the headphones, he would be happy. Aaron's stomach knotted, and he said a silent prayer that the doctor wouldn't try to disrupt Max's peace.

"Hello, hello!" the doctor said, entering the room as if on cue. Standing at six foot six, Dr. Hancock exuded the youthful energy of a former athlete. Aaron and Diana sat up a little straighter. While Aaron looked at the doctor skeptically, Diana put on her best smile. Already, her intuition said he would be wonderful with her two younger sons, but the boom of his voice indicated that he wasn't aware that Max had autism—or if he was, that he wasn't aware of the impact of loud noises on so many of these children. She hoped that her instincts were off and that Max would like him, too. If this went poorly, it would be the fastest "I told you so" Aaron had ever said.

Dr. Hancock took a step over to Max, who had already turned his attention back to his iPad. "You must be Max," he said loudly, trying to speak over Max's headphones. "I'm Dr. Hancock." His forehead wrinkled when Max didn't respond.

"He has autism," Diana said quietly.

"Oh. Of course." Dr. Hancock took a seat on the tall stool in the corner of the room. He ran a hand through his chestnut-colored hair, which shone in the fluorescent lights. "How can I help you folks today?" he asked, smiling.

Aaron shifted. Diana could feel his hackles rising, and she put her hand on his knee while looking at him with eyes that said, "You promised to try this." Aaron took a deep breath and smiled back at the doctor.

"We've been treating Max's ASD with natural supplements and nutrition since he was diagnosed," Diana explained. "Everything was manageable until a few months ago. Max became more physically aggressive, and since he's getting stronger than me . . ." Diana trailed off. "Well, we're ready to try a more traditional medical approach, and we've come to you for recommendations."

Dr. Hancock smiled at her. "I'm glad you did. It's my pleasure to work with your family. Frankly, after reviewing Max's medical records from Dr. Peterson, I'm surprised it took you so long to come to the 'dark side.'" He chuckled, pleased with his own joke about Western medicine. Seeing that Aaron and Diana weren't amused, he continued. "What I'd like to try are medications that other children with autism have experienced success with."

"Okay," Diana said. "What are those?"

"Autism is such a complex disorder that there isn't *one* pill I can use to treat it. I'm sure, as you've taken an alternative therapeutic approach, that you're aware of all the intricacies of the disorder. Can you tell me more about Max's behavior over the past few months?" Dr. Hancock removed a small pad and pen from his inside jacket pocket, poised to take notes. His studious posture came so naturally that Diana couldn't help wondering how long he'd been out of med school.

Diana launched into a reply, ending her thorough history with the previous day's conference with Max's principal. She was surprised but pleased with herself for making the story concise and matter of fact.

"I see. So, the main problems that you're experiencing with Max are uncontrollable meltdowns and a high level of distractibility?" Dr. Hancock looked up from his file.

"That's about right," Diana said, nodding.

"I don't know. He seems pretty calm right now to me. Other patients with autism . . ." Dr. Hancock trailed off as he eyed the boy perched calmly on the exam table. "But I can't even begin to imagine the struggles that brought you here." He cleared his throat. "I'm going to give you a mood stabilizer, which is a psychotropic medication that should help with aggression, impulsivity, and self-injury."

Psychotropic medications, such as mood stabilizers, may be prescribed as part of comprehensive treatment for ASD. Different medical providers can prescribe psychotropic medications. Which provider prescribes psychotropic medications for each individual depends on a number of factors, including training, experience, availability of specialists, and response to treatment. The following is a list of trained providers who may prescribe psychotropic medications:

a. A *psychiatrist* (M.D.) or *child and adolescent psychiatrist* (M.D.) is an individual with a medical degree (M.D.), licensed by individual states to practice psychiatry. They specialize in providing evaluations and treating emotional and behavioral problems and mental disorders by prescribing psychotropic medications and with other psychotherapeutic techniques.

b. A *pediatrician* (M.D.) is an individual licensed by the state. They specialize in treating the general medical problems of newborns, infants, children, and adolescents. Some pediatricians may prescribe psychotropic medications depending on the availability of psychiatrists and each one's comfort level.

c. A *nurse practitioner* (N.P. or A.P.N.P.) is an individual licensed by the state, who has either a master's degree or doctorate degree. He or she is a registered nurse who has acquired the knowledge base, decision-making skills, and clinical competencies for expanded practice beyond that of an R.N., the characteristics of which would be determined by the context in which he or she is credentialed to practice. They may specialize in various fields of medicine, including psychiatry and pediatrics. They typically work in conjunction with a physician (M.D.).

d. A *physician's assistant* (P.A.) is an individual licensed by the state, who has completed a master's degree. He or she practices medicine on a team under the supervision of physicians (M.D.). They are formally educated to examine patients, diagnose injuries and illnesses, and provide treatment.

Aaron felt Diana looking at him, but he avoided her gaze. He hated the thought of his son on medication. He was only twelve! A little boy still. Dr. Hancock made it sound as though Max would take this pill and everything would be better—but there was so much they didn't know about how Max would react and what the long-term effects on his body might be. Aaron had always believed that if you treated the upstream causes, the downstream effects would naturally improve (he drank water when he had a headache, for example, rather than taking acetaminophen or naproxen, which were tough on the liver). He'd been telling himself that for eight years. But Diana was right: nothing had changed, and Max was only going to get older, bigger, and stronger. Aaron knew he owed it not only to Max but to their entire family to give this a chance. But he couldn't pretend he agreed with the approach. In fact, it terrified him.

Dr. Hancock ripped a page from his prescription pad and handed it to Diana. "I think you're going to see a marked change in Max, and soon," he said. "The autism road is tough to navigate. No matter how well intentioned natural or holistic remedies may be, the only positive changes in autistic youth we have seen are with evidence-based treatment."

> *Evidence-based treatment* generally includes (a) clinical expertise and expert opinion, (b) external scientific evidence, and (c) client, patient, and caregiver perspectives to provide high-quality services reflecting the interests, values, needs, and choices of the individuals served.

Diana gave the doctor a tight smile while Aaron felt the blow go straight to his chest. The pediatrician had implied, maybe inadvertently, that they'd been going about Max's treatment wrong all along. Aaron's belly burned with indignation but sank with the feeling that the doctor was right, or they wouldn't be here in the first place.

"What about side effects?" Aaron blurted. He tried to keep the defensive tone out of his voice. "What should we be looking out for?"

> Every medication, including over-the-counter (OTC) medication, has the potential for *side effects*. Working closely with a physician can minimize the chance of experiencing significant side effects. Remember, most medication side effects are mild and occur only during the first few days of starting a new medication or increasing the dose.

Diana gave him a cautionary glance, but he ignored it. Just because they were going to feed Max drugs didn't mean they shouldn't still try to protect him—and if it didn't occur to Diana to ask these questions, he sure as hell would.

Dr. Hancock ticked off a casual list on his fingers. "Oh, you might see some stomach upset, maybe some sleeplessness, possibly some weight gain or loss. I'll give you another prescription for a sleep aid, just in case you find that to be an issue. If you see Max seeming depressed or more self-injurious than usual, give me a call right away. Otherwise, I suggest you keep a journal of any changes you see in Max's behavior.

All in all, though, parents typically find that side effects are minor and worth the improvements." He smiled.

For whom? Aaron wanted to ask. It made him sick to think of parents medicating their children to make their own lives easier, rather than to actually help the kids. But this time, he stayed quiet.

After helping Max get buckled in the backseat, Aaron shifted the car into reverse to drop off Max's new prescriptions at the local pharmacy.

"How are you feeling?" Diana asked quietly.

"I don't know," Aaron said. He kept his eyes on the road. "Either like I've wasted eight years or like I've compromised. Either way I'm failing him."

Diana put her hand on Aaron's forearm. She hadn't even considered how his ego might play into this. "You're a wonderful father, Aaron," she said. "If you weren't, you wouldn't care—you wouldn't try as hard as you have to help him. You wouldn't be concerned about medicating him. A bad father would just want this problem kid out of his hair. Just being supportive of me and this new approach proves how much you care about doing what's best for our son.

"Besides," she continued, "it's not as though all the hard work and research that you've done is for nothing. We're keeping his dietary restrictions intact. We're going to work with the over-the-counter supplements that we can find. I feel good about this, Aaron. Dr. Hancock was confident that we'd made the right call, and while obviously I'm nervous, I at least feel that we have an entire world of untapped resources available. Things are going to get better." Diana dropped her hand from Aaron's arm and interlaced her fingers with his. He glanced at her and rewarded her with a small smile.

Yeah, he wanted to say. That's what I thought, too.

. . .

Diana sat wearily in front of the computer screen and realized that she'd not retained a single piece of information from the staff meeting she'd just left. She was creating a press kit for the nonprofit's annual fundraising gala, and she was thankful that she'd taken notes on everything that Rosey, the executive director, had discussed. She and Rosey had been sorority sisters, but while Diana had married Aaron at twenty-four, when he was still in dental school, Rosey had gone on to graduate school and had built her own agency. While Rosey knew that Diana had a knack for public relations, she'd started her friend out slow since Diana hadn't worked in almost thirteen years. Now, however, she was pushing Diana to lead the campaign for the biggest event of the year. Diana didn't want to let Rosey down. She knew she could do the work, find the professional fulfillment that she hadn't even had time to miss amid the dirty diapers and rowdy boys who had taken up the past decade and a half. But she knew instinctively that now wasn't the time many mothers experienced, when the children were school-age and a career could be resurrected. Things were more complex than that.

Almost immediately after starting the medication three weeks earlier, Max's mood and behavior had shifted. His language had increased, and he was more emotionally expressive, but his temper seemed to overwhelm him. Putting him to bed at night had become a taxing chore, resulting in Max rising and coming into Aaron and Diana's room almost every hour on the hour. When Aaron or Diana tried to lead him back to bed, he yelled so furiously that his younger brothers woke up. Once, Aiden had come to Diana's room and, sounding far wearier than a child should, asked, "Is Max *ever* going to get better?" Max's tantrums had been bad enough a few months ago, but Diana wondered whether her son was getting stronger; he looked as though he'd put on some weight. The entire family was exhausted, and Diana's anxiety rose as she considered that perhaps the medication was making Max worse instead of better. But this was the path she'd chosen, the path she believed would best serve Max; so, rather than focus on her fears, she dove into her notes and journaling of Max's behavior. She took the task so seriously that she was deeply startled that afternoon when the phone rang.

"Hello?" she answered, misplaced adrenaline making her heart pound.

"Hello, Diana." Mrs. Deveraux's voice was strained.

"Hi, Mrs. Deveraux. Is everything okay?"

"I'm afraid not. I'm going to have to ask you to come and get Max again," she said. "His teacher is here in the office. She can talk with you about what's happened."

Diana closed her eyes for a moment. It was so bad that Mrs. Deveraux wouldn't even tell her what had happened until she got there? "Is Max okay?" she asked brusquely.

She was already shutting down her computer, stomach in knots.

"He's with the nurse," Mrs. Deveraux said. "He seems okay now."

"Thank you," Diana said, gathering her purse. "I'll see you soon."

She stuck her head into Rosey's office on her way out. Rosey looked up from her computer.

"Max," Diana said.

Rosey made a sympathetic face, but Diana knew her friend was also thinking about the gala campaign.

"I'll be in first thing after dropping the boys off tomorrow," Diana said before Rosey had a chance to respond. This was becoming a habit of hers, she realized—cutting off objection at the pass with a reassurance or promise or request. She didn't like it very much.

Rosey waved her off. "Of course. Go do what you need to do."

In the principal's office, Mrs. Deveraux sat with Isabella Carrita, Max's teacher. Mrs. Carrita's gray-green eyes were swollen and puffy, her mascaraed lashes clumpy with tears.

"Hi." Diana walked in and took a seat without waiting for an invitation. "Max is still with the nurse?" she asked.

"We thought it best to leave him there so that we could talk," Mrs. Deveraux responded.

"Okay," Diana said, biting her lip. "So, what happened?"

Mrs. Carrita gave her a thin smile. "You know how much I care about Max, which is why the last incident, when he hurt himself, threw me off guard so much. I'd never seen him so self-injurious before. Today was even worse than that."

Mrs. Carrita explained how Max had asked to use the restroom, which he hadn't done all week. The restroom was connected to the classroom, and when Mrs. Carrita gave him permission, Max locked himself inside. When ten minutes passed, Mrs. Carrita discreetly knocked on the door—she didn't want to embarrass him in front of his classmates, she explained, but ten minutes was enough time for concern. He didn't answer, but she heard the sound of thumping from inside, a repetitive, dull *thwack, thwack, thwack.* Immediately, she'd thought of the last time, poor Max throwing his head against the wall, and she moved to call a male aide to check on Max. That was when something crashed inside the bathroom—breaking glass. Mrs. Carrita ran to find Mr. Valentine, who opened the bathroom to find Max bruised and bloody and stunned. He must have been banging his forehead against the mirror, Mrs. Carrita said, her voice cracking. Max was crumpled on the floor beside the broken glass, and when Mr. Valentine tried to pull him up, Max went wild. He was screaming and kicking and thrashing, so much so that Mr. Valentine yelled at Mrs. Carrita to get the other kids out of the room.

"They're both okay," Mrs. Carrita finished. "I mean, as okay as they can be. But Max might need stitches. You should take him to a doctor right away."

"My God," Diana said. Her mouth tasted coppery, and she realized she'd bitten her lip hard enough to draw blood. "I'm so sorry." The apology was reflexive; it came in grocery stores and restaurants, on sidewalks and playgrounds. Max should just wear a shirt, she thought bitterly, that said My Mother Is Sorry. Immediately, a rush of guilt followed. Her son needed *stitches,* for Christ's sake.

He'd broken a mirror with his *head*. Why was she apologizing for him when she should be comforting him?

Diana started to stand but froze in an awkward crouch. "Wait—you said Max hasn't asked to use the restroom all week?"

"Um. No. He hasn't. Which is unusual for him," Mrs. Carrita said, looking stumped.

Diana sighed and sat back down. "We started him on new medication three weeks ago. We didn't want to tell you at first—I'm not sure why. But I wonder if it could be making him constipated . . ." Diana trailed off slightly. "If it has, he's probably really uncomfortable and can't express it. That kind of frustration was a big trigger for his self-injurious behavior in the past." A new wave of Mad Mom Guilt rose to her chest as she spoke, making her feel claustrophobic. Why hadn't she noticed, put two and two together? If she'd been paying more attention, she could have prevented Max from hurting himself. "I'm taking him back to the pediatrician. This—medicating him—is a new thing for us. I'm so sorry for his behavior, but we're doing the best we can at home. I promise."

"I'm sure you are," Mrs. Deveraux replied reassuringly.

Diana released a breath she hadn't realized she was holding. "I should take him home now," she said, standing to shake both women's hands.

"Yes, you should. And remember," Mrs. Carrita said, her voice lifting, "tomorrow is a new day."

Diana smiled, wishing she shared the optimism.

• • •

In Dr. Hancock's waiting room, Diana tried to hold an ice-pack to Max's face despite his squirming and screaming each time her hand came near him. When they finally got to the exam room, Max was frantic, yelling and pulling at the white paper on the exam table. Diana used all her strength to wrap him in her arms, preventing him from throwing his body against the walls. Finally, Max settled on the floor, where he sat cross-legged and rocking, though his mouth was twisted in an expression of distress as he wailed. Dr. Hancock walked into the room a minute later, blinking at the sight. For a moment, Diana saw her son through the doctor's eyes: a boy on the cusp of adolescence, pushing a hundred and twenty pounds, whom one might otherwise expect to see on the soccer field or scrolling through Facebook or Instagram—swollen forehead, wailing, rocking the way a toddler throwing a tantrum might. Diana knew her son. Max was simply Max to her. But to others, who learned he had autism after initially thinking he was "normal," it was cognitive dissonance.

"Hey, buddy," Dr. Hancock said loudly to Max. "We could hear you three rooms down. What's going on?"

"Well, he just got four stitches at urgent care," Diana said, trying to keep accusation out of her voice. "He decided to break a mirror with his head today. We need to discuss these medications."

Dr. Hancock leaned down to look at Max, but Max thrashed and tried to headbutt him. Dr. Hancock stepped back, palms out conciliatorily. "Well, the stitches look good," he said, moving across the room, closer to Diana. "They shouldn't leave much of a scar. I'm sorry to hear about this, though. Now, what about the medicines?"

"Well, clearly they're not working!" Diana said, gesturing toward Max with exasperation. "They were supposed to reduce his self-injurious behavior, but instead they've made him severely constipated—at least that's my suspicion—which has made him out of control. He could have really hurt himself today!" Diana's voice broke before she continued briskly, "And he's put on almost ten pounds. In just a few weeks. That doesn't seem normal or healthy to me."

"Hmm. I see. It sounds like we need to try something else." Dr. Hancock reached for his prescription pad and wrote out two new prescriptions. "Let's try a different mood stabilizer, plus a stimulant. Until the constipation gets better, give him a nonstimulating laxative daily." He handed her the prescriptions. "I'd like to see him again in a month." The doctor gave a slight wave as he walked out the door. "See you, Max."

> **Stimulants** are a type of psychotropic medication that induce temporary improvements in mental or physical function or both. Stimulants are often prescribed for symptom reduction in children, adolescents, and adults with attention deficit hyperactivity disorder, among other mental disorders.

"Wait!" Diana called. Dr. Hancock turned around in the doorway. "That's it? I mean—"

Max's wails were unrelenting, a blend of high-pitched mewling and deeper, throatier yells. Every so often, his breath caught in a childlike hiccup before he opened his mouth and screamed even louder. Diana's head was throbbing, and she blinked away her own tears of frustration and fear. How many times had they been caught in this awful dance? Max completely out of control, she sweating and silently begging and swearing, trying to remove her son from a room without causing further hysteria, and still for some reason—futilely—trying to avoid the judgment of other parents. "Never mind," she said to the doctor, trying to keep her composure as she pulled Max up by his elbow. "Come on, Max. Let's get you home."

When she got Max into the car, he finally stopped screaming. He sat quietly in the backseat, his face looking almost misshapen from the injury and the crying. He stared out the window, and Diana wondered, as she always wondered, what he was thinking. The heartbreak of ASD was that so often, the tools she had as a mother to her other sons—the ability to intuit their feelings, to understand how to soothe them—didn't translate with Max. It was as though they sat back to back, and while she could feel the warmth of his skin, she couldn't see his eyes or what lay beyond them. And if she, his own mother, didn't understand him, how could anybody else? How could Max ever be anything but alone?

CHAPTER 3

Diana was pulling the pot roast from the oven when she realized she'd spent fifteen minutes in the kitchen without hearing anything from her boys. Growing suspicious, she peeked her head into their bedrooms, starting with her youngest son's. Aiden and Justin were immersed in playing with Star Wars action figures on the floor.

"Boom! I'm going to get you, Luke!" Justin did his best James Earl Jones as he held the Darth Vader figure over the blue lightsaber. Diana smiled before slipping her head back through the door. Across the hall, she was surprised to hear nothing behind Max's closed door. Cracking it open, she saw her son sitting at the foot of his bed, arms limp at his sides, staring at the wall.

"Max. Baby," she said, walking into the room. "What are you doing?"

He didn't acknowledge her. That wasn't unusual, but when Max ignored her, he was usually busying himself with something else. Right now he just looked so . . . vacant. Gently, Diana took a seat beside him.

"Max?" she asked again, putting her hand on his arm. He turned his head with the contact and gave a half smile, but his oceanic eyes looked right through her.

"Do you want to eat?" she asked, stroking his forehead.

Max looked around the room, as if he knew there was an answer but couldn't figure out what it was. He put a hand to his belly. "Hungry?" he asked.

Diana nodded. Something was really off. Max had been on his new medication for about a month. At first, she'd been thrilled at the changes: his constipation had cleared up with help from the laxative, and his mood had improved so that meltdowns and self-injury had become rare. But in the last week or so, he'd reminded Diana of a little snail, curling further and further inward. While he'd always had trouble socially connecting and communicating, now he seemed *absent*, devoid of feelings. No laughter, no physical contact with anyone, no enjoyment derived from his extensive music collection or DVDs. The appointment with Dr. Hancock was scheduled for the following day, and although Diana wasn't happy with the quality of care he'd provided, she didn't know who else she could turn to. She wished they could get something in the middle of the aggressive, hurting boy she'd brought in a month ago and the zombie she was living with now. She held her son by the elbow, gently guiding him from the bed and leading him down the hallway to the dining table. She seated him at the head and then went to call her other sons for dinner.

When Aaron returned home from work a few minutes later, he found his family sitting at the table, but the air was heavy. He set down his bag and joined them, realizing why the house felt so strange: no one was speaking. Typically, when he got home just in time for dinner, Diana was wrangling the boys to the table or trying to calm them down. Aiden was usually upset that his mother had interrupted his play, while Justin was trying to tell her all about his science class. Max would join the fray, sometimes laughing and sometimes wailing, but the three of them were never this quiet. The younger boys sat with their hands in their laps and their eyes searching for an answer. Max stared at the pine of the dining table, oblivious to everything. The fist of discomfort that had lodged itself in Aaron's chest since Max's first visit with the pediatrician hardened. *This*—this was *exactly* what he'd been trying to avoid: Max looked like the stereotypical drugged-up patient in some institution. All he was missing was a spot of drool.

"Hi, sweetie," Diana said. She was watching his face, which he now carefully rearranged into an expression of cheer for the boys.

"Dinner sure smells good!" he said. He smiled, and Justin and Aiden grinned back at him. "How are my little men?"

Justin and Aiden nodded in response, but Max continued to stare at the table. Aaron helped Diana make plates for the boys and then took his seat. It was the quietest meal the family had ever shared. Aaron would trade it in a heartbeat, he thought, for Max yelling about the meat juice touching his mashed potatoes. Aaron realized that this was his biggest fear: that they would lose the pieces of Max they had to medication.

After the longest dinner Aaron could remember, the younger boys went off to their rooms to finish their homework, and Aaron began Max's evening ritual, starting with a shower. When he walked back into his own room, he saw Diana lying on top of the bedcovers, staring at the ceiling.

"What the hell did I do?" she said, not looking at him. "I just wanted what was best for him. I didn't mean to turn him into a zombie. Maybe you were right. Maybe we shouldn't have touched the stuff. I don't know. I'm at a total loss."

Aaron sat at the foot of the bed. How easy it would be to blame her, to let her languish in guilt in hopes it would relieve his own. Instead, clipped, he said, "We're going back to the doctor tomorrow. We'll see what he says. If we're not in alignment, we'll explore other options."

Diana nodded and rolled over, peeling back the covers and slipping beneath them. She curled into a ball, facing away from him, and Aaron stared at her shoulder blades under her t-shirt. She'd lost weight over the past six weeks, but it didn't look like a healthy slimming down. She looked tired and slightly malnourished. He wanted to reach over and comfort her, but that would require more energy than he had right now. He should have been able to fix this, for all of them, but he couldn't ease his wife's suffering with a touch any more than he could cure Max's disorder with kale and fish oil. He sighed and quietly picked up the novel he was reading before leaving Diana alone on their bed.

...

The next night, Diana slipped on her reading glasses and pulled up a search engine on her laptop. She had three new prescriptions before her, and before she started Max on them the following morning, she had decided to do some additional research. Dr. Hancock had again been in a hurry. While he jotted down the new medications, Max had sat serenely on the exam table, his eyes glazed. At the last minute, Aaron had been unable to make the appointment and Diana was glad; she didn't think he'd be able to stop himself from tearing into the young doctor, despite his best intentions.

At the end of the visit, Dr. Hancock had said, "You know, if we don't see success with this next attempt, it might be a good idea for you to see a psychiatrist." Diana had gaped at him. *Really?* she almost asked. *Now* you tell me this? While she appreciated Dr. Hancock's willingness to admit, however indirectly, that he was not an expert on treatment for autism, why hadn't he recommended a psychiatrist on their first visit? Why would it take two— possibly three—painful attempts at medicating her son before he referred her to someone with greater expertise in this area? Still, she couldn't help a sense of desperate hope. *What if* this next round of medication got it right? There was a chance, wasn't there?

The first new medication was the least familiar to her, so she started there, typing the brand name of the prescription into the search engine. The picture that popped up showed little white pills that were identical to the ones lying on the bottom of the prescription bottle. However, the description underneath had to be incorrect. She scrolled down and clicked on the manufacturer's website, and her stomach dropped. This medication was primarily used to treat hypertension, with a secondary effect of some mood stabilization. Just as she made that discovery, Aaron walked into their bedroom.

> **Antihypertensive medications** are a group of medications originally designed to treat those with hypertension (high blood pressure). Much like aspirin, which was originally designed to treat pain and is now used for other medical purposes (including to help prevent heart attacks and strokes), antihypertensives are also used for other reasons, including behavioral difficulties (such as physical and verbal aggression, impulsivity) and attention deficit hyperactivity disorder.

"What's going on?" he asked, seeing the incredulous look on her face.

"A blood pressure medication!" she practically exclaimed.

"What?" Aaron was confused.

"That's Max's newest drug. A blood pressure medication." She sighed. "Are we doing the right thing?" she asked Aaron, her eyes begging for an indication that he was with her, even if this hadn't been his first choice.

Just yesterday, he'd been able to offer her some comfort, but tonight, he simply left the room and went to Max's bedroom. Aaron sat on the edge of the bed, next to his son, and stroked the dark hair that had fallen on his forehead. Max's skin was slippery with sleep-sweat, and Aaron could smell the remnants of the Dial soap that his son had used to shower a few hours ago. He leaned in and kissed Max's forehead.

"I promise we're going to figure this out," Aaron whispered in the dark.

Returning to his bedroom, Aaron found Diana in tears on their bed. She sat up and swiped a hand under her nose when she saw him. Diana had always hated to let anyone see her cry.

"We need to move on from Dr. Hancock," Aaron said firmly. "He may be a great pediatrician for kids with strep throat or the flu, but Max is different. We'll regroup with a child psychiatrist as soon as possible, but in the meantime, I'm no longer going to watch my son vary between Dr. Jekyll and Mr. Hyde. We'll just stop giving him the meds."

Diana opened her mouth, but Aaron held up a hand.

"Look," he said, "I know the natural treatment didn't

do much, but at least it didn't seem to *harm* him. We tried it your way, but let's face it—the pediatrician angle didn't work."

Diana looked at Aaron as if he'd lost his mind. "We can't just *stop* giving him those medications. He has to be weaned off—"

> Like many medications, psychotropic medications can result in symptoms if they are decreased or stopped abruptly. These symptoms differ depending on the medication. They can be quite uncomfortable, but are not typically dangerous unless the medication is a benzodiazepine (such as clonazepam, lorazepam, alprazolam). Remember to never alter or stop any medication unless you first consult with your physician.

"What, like he was weaned off the first mood stabilizer before he started the second?" Aaron retorted. "Dr. Hancock didn't ask us to taper. What difference would it make?"

Diana's entire body grew even more tense, which she hadn't known was possible. She wanted what was best for Max, but she didn't feel comfortable interfering with the medication that Dr. Hancock had prescribed. Yet, Aaron had a point: they *hadn't* been asked to wean Max off the first mood stabilizer before trying the second. What harm could it do to have Max without medication for a few days while they scheduled an appointment with a psychiatrist? That way, the psychiatrist would get to see Max for who he was, without the influence of psychotropic drugs. She looked up. Aaron's dark eyes shone in anticipation of her answer.

"I do see your point," she said slowly, "but we're not doctors. I'll call a psychiatrist tomorrow and see what they recommend."

"*I'm* a doctor, Diana," Aaron said, flopping down on the bed next to his wife.

"You're a dentist!" she exclaimed. "You know nothing about anything other than the kinds of painkillers and antibiotics that you prescribe after root canals! Nothing about psychotropic medications!"

Aaron's eyes were hurt. "You know what?" he said. "You're doing such a great job, you handle it!" He turned his back to Diana, trying to remember his yoga breath to ease the roaring in his ears.

Diana wiped her eyes and forced the tears back. She didn't know what was right or wrong anymore. She'd never felt more powerless. And she hated fighting with Aaron. The *only* thing that had made this journey with Max bearable was their partnership. If they were on opposing sides . . . Diana shook her head, staring at her husband's back. She wanted to reach out and touch him, but she could feel his anger radiating. She was afraid he'd shake her off, rejecting her. That would be worse still.

Sighing, she grabbed her laptop and padded to the living room, where she settled beneath a blanket on the couch. Then she searched for withdrawal symptoms for the medications that Max was currently on. The results made her shudder. There were stories of how some children had become so anxious that they didn't sleep for over twenty-four hours. Some children cried uncontrollably, while others were nauseated and dizzy, unable to move from their beds. Worst yet, some children even became psychotic. She couldn't imagine putting her son or her other children through that kind of hell, especially after all they'd been through over the past six months. Diana knew she couldn't win: she had to choose between what Aaron thought was best, and what her gut—and now her logic—was screaming at her. She wouldn't stop Max's meds cold turkey. She couldn't.

Back in their bedroom, Aaron had already fallen asleep. He snored softly, his cheeks puffing a little as he exhaled. Diana remembered the first time that she'd seen him sleeping. He'd come to her parents' house for Thanksgiving her junior year of college, and after playing football with her brothers and cousins, he'd fallen asleep in front of the Packers game, too full and exhausted to do anything other than snooze on the couch. They hadn't been together long then, but when she heard the soft buzz of his sleeping breath, she knew she wanted to hear that every night for the rest of her life. When Max was a baby, his chubby cheeks puffed in the same way as his father's. She had a picture of them in bed together, sleeping in the same position. She'd captioned it "Foolproof Paternity Test" and emailed it to all of their family and friends. Max was certainly Aaron's, but he was hers, too. In the same way that she'd had to explain that she was no longer comfortable with an entirely natural approach to Max's care, she had to stand firm now, no matter what that meant. Max deserved more than he'd had, but she was going to work with a doctor to ensure that they got there.

Diana didn't tell Aaron before she gave Max his new medication the next morning. She dreaded the conversation too much. While a part of her knew that avoiding difficult conversations with Aaron could be the first slip down a long spiral, she couldn't bring herself to do otherwise.

Aaron left for work without a word. Since she wasn't going into the office, she ran errands, saying silent prayers with every inch her car took her down the highway. Maybe this time Max's medications would work. Maybe this time things would be different for her family. She stared straight ahead, taking comfort in familiar routes.

CHAPTER 4

Diana yawned and fell back onto her bed. It was three a.m. and the second week in a row that she'd slept fewer than three hours a night. Her mind felt soggy and waterlogged. She'd driven off with her cup of coffee on the roof of her car the other day; it had taken her three hours yesterday to write a simple press release. She didn't remember nursing a newborn as being this taxing.

Since Aaron was out of town at an anesthesia conference, she'd handled all three boys on her own all week, and Max's medication changes couldn't have come at a worse time. For the past nine nights, Max had come into her bedroom and screamed in her face until she woke up. She could hear him when he started now, his wails echoing off the hardwood floors in the hallway that connected all the bedrooms. Knowing that he was keeping his younger brothers up, she'd tried everything to comfort him, but he was irrational, angrily smacking her hands away if she tried to touch him. For a moment, in her sleep-deprived haze, she'd considered just locking him in his room. He was inconsolable, and at least that way maybe everyone could get some sleep. But that was crazy. She crawled back into bed. It seemed like no time at all had passed when she heard a slight knock at her door.

"Mom?" Justin's little voice filled her room as he peeked his head in through the door.

"Yes, baby?" she asked, not knowing when she'd fallen asleep. She blinked. Her eyes were so dry.

"It's . . . it's time to get up for school," Justin said apologetically. "We need you to drive us."

Diana glanced at the clock. Six-thirty a.m. "Okay, buddy. Can you give me just a minute?"

"Aiden and I took showers last night. We just have to get dressed. I'll make us some cereal," he offered.

Diana propped herself up on her elbow and looked at her middle son. Waves of guilt crashed over her. She should get up. She should make them a real breakfast. But she was so tired.

"Take a nap," Justin said, smiling bravely at his mom. "I'll wake you up in thirty minutes. I know you were up with Max again last night."

Diana's heart melted with the little considerate soul before her. "Thank you, baby. Please come get me when you're ready. I'm so sorry," she said, half feeling like the worst mom in the world for letting her nine- and seven-year-olds get themselves ready for school, and half feeling like the best for raising young men who could take such initiative. She didn't have long to consider how she felt, for as soon as her head lowered again, she fell into a deep, anxious sleep.

"Mommy!" She wasn't sure why Aiden was coming to the tea party with the Backstreet Boys and Glenn Beck. "Mommy!" he cried again. Weird, she thought, before little hands were shaking her from behind. "Mommy! Max is trying to kill Justin! Get up!"

"What?" Diana sat straight up and put her feet on the

floor, heart racing. "What's happening?" she asked, instantly made awake by the terror in her youngest son's eyes.

"Come!" Aiden said, pulling her from her bedroom. She followed him in a half jog to find her kitchen destroyed and Max on top of Justin. For a moment, her mind made sense of it as boys wrestling—playing. But Justin's face was a mottled purple, his eyes bulging in shock as he clawed at Max's arms and tried to buck the larger boy off him.

"Max!" Diana shouted. "Get off your brother!" She grabbed Max by the bicep and yanked him toward her, but his grip was tight. Trying a different tack, she shoved Max to the side, and when he toppled over, Justin gasped and scrambled away. "Mom!" he cried, coughing and touching his throat. The expression on his face was hurt surprise, as though he just couldn't believe his brother would do that to him. When Diana stooped down to examine her middle child, Max charged her from behind. She fell straight on her chest, knocking her chin on the wood floor. Max dug a knee into her back, pulling Diana's hair.

"Mommy!" Aiden cried from across the room.

Diana tried to breathe as Justin jumped up and grabbed the phone. Distantly, she heard him giving their address and saying, "He has autism, he's really big, and we can't control him." Diana placed her palms by her chest in pushup position, took a deep breath, and rolled herself over, grasping for Max at the same time. He yelled, "No, no, no!" and slapped her, hard, across the face. Six months ago, when he'd acted out similarly, she'd had trouble holding her own against him, but now that he'd gained weight, it was even harder. Adrenaline and fear for her other sons kept her exhausted and overwhelmed body moving.

"Go to my bedroom!" she cried out to her younger sons. "I'll be right there!"

She heard the boys scamper down the hallway and turned around to get on her feet. Max was behind her, his face blotched red as he charged her again. She jumped out of his way, and he hit his head on the kitchen counter. A swift rush of maternal guilt made her nauseated, but she couldn't check to make sure he hadn't hurt himself right now. She ran into the bedroom with Justin and Aiden and locked the door behind her as the sounds of yelling and banging reverberated from the kitchen. Max must be throwing his head against the countertop or table.

"Oh, God," Diana said out loud. Every instinct made her want to run out again and save Max from himself, but if something happened to her, what would Justin and Aiden do? She felt as if she were choosing between her children, and any move she might make was impossible and damning.

It occurred to her then to call Aaron, but Justin and Aiden had pressed themselves against her, crying into her ribs. She rubbed their backs, repeating, "It's okay, it's okay," as she listened to the sounds of Max's undirected rage. If she could still hear him, she reassured herself, he was okay.

The doorbell rang, breaking the cadence of Max's banging. She kissed both boys' heads. "Stay right here. Keep the door locked," she told them, before rushing across the crime scene of her living room and to the foyer, where she unlocked the front door. "He's in the kitchen," she said, hardly recognizing her own voice.

The two officers saw Max and rushed towards him.

One was able to cuff him while he writhed and thrashed. She watched it all like a movie. This wasn't her life. It couldn't be. Max threw himself to the ground in the cuffs, crying loudly. She knew that his wrists hurt. That he was confused. That he didn't mean it.

"Hey! He's just a child!" she cried out when the officer tried to pick Max up, leading his squirming body up to his knees.

"I know," the officer responded, the deep lines in his forehead indicating that his actions broke his heart. "We just have to restrain him until the paramedics arrive to make sure he doesn't hurt anyone, including himself."

Diana ran to her son and knelt beside him so that they were nose to nose. "Max, it's going to be okay. I promise."

Max stared at a point above her right shoulder.

"Max," she tried again. "We love you so much."

Max tipped his head backwards and threw it into hers as hard as he could. Her vision blackened, fragmenting into stars as she fell back. Involuntary tears streamed down her face as the officer helped her up and led her to the couch. Just as she was seated, she heard someone enter. She turned to see a young paramedic administering a shot into Max's arm as he thrashed about, and Max was loaded onto a stretcher while the police officer sat next to Diana, his hazel eyes heavy with concern.

> Some psychotropic medications have an injectable form available that is injected into a muscle. These medications are typically the antipsychotic medications. Your physician may recommend an injectable form of a medication if your loved one has difficulty being compliant with oral medications and has significant symptoms. Injectable medications may also be used if someone is acutely agitated and aggressive and poses a threat of hurting themselves or others.

"The paramedics are taking him to Ridgeview Hospital," he said. "If you'd like, you can follow him. However, I wouldn't recommend . . ." He trailed off, nodding towards her bedroom door. Justin and Aiden were huddled together, watching their brother's unconscious body being carefully strapped onto the wooden stretcher.

Diana had completely forgotten about her other sons. "I'll call a neighbor and meet Max at Ridgeview. I need to call my husband."

The police officer put his hand on Diana's. "Your son will be fine at the hospital until you figure out what you need to do. That sedative will last for a while. You might also want to get dressed."

Diana realized that she was still only wearing her oversized t-shirt, which barely came to the tops of her thighs. Hot with embarrassment, she pulled the hem and crossed her arms over her chest. The police officer blushed a little and smiled sadly at her as he walked toward the front door.

• • •

"We're looking at a seventy-two hour stay due to the severity of the behavior and medication history. We need to ensure that he's emotionally and behaviorally stable, especially considering that he has younger brothers in the home," the psychiatrist said, looking at Diana sympathetically.

> Emergency detention is typically a *seventy-two hour period* of involuntary detention of an individual in a psychiatric unit for emergency evaluation if someone, as a result of a mental disorder, presents a clear and present danger to (a) self, (b) others, or (c) is gravely disabled and unable to care for him- or herself or organize basic necessities. While admitted, treatment is begun and may include psychotropic medications.

She nodded, trying to take everything in. She'd called her neighbor, who'd picked up Justin and Aiden, and Aaron was catching the next flight in from Detroit. He'd promised to be with her by dinnertime.

"He's still sedated, but when he wakes, we will do a thorough evaluation. I'll have more news for you then, but for now, please try to get some rest." The lanyard around the psychiatrist's neck caught the fluorescent light, and Dr. Jefferson's name and photo shined on his badge. His bright red, bald head caught the same light.

Diana forced a tight smile. She wasn't sure what else to do, so she stood to leave the hospital.

Her drive home was dazed, automatic. She knew she should pick up her younger boys, but she just didn't have the physical or emotional capacity to answer questions and comfort them right now. She pulled into her garage and fell into her bed with her shoes on.

Three hours later, Aaron crawled into bed beside her. She awoke as the bed shifted under his weight, and she tensed, prepared for a fight. Instead, Aaron wrapped his arms around her from behind and kissed the top of her head. She didn't open her eyes, and within moments, she was sleeping again.

Diana awoke to total darkness. She looked at the clock on her bedside table: six a.m. Frantically, she jumped up. She'd slept all night. What about Aiden and Justin? Then she heard their little voices, along with Aaron's, and breathed a sigh of relief. He'd taken care of them. She walked toward the bedroom door and tripped over the sandals that Aaron must have removed from her feet sometime in the previous fifteen hours.

She found her husband and young sons cuddled on

48

the living room couch. He had his arms around both boys, and they were speaking in hushed tones.

"Hi, Mom," Justin said when he noticed her standing in the doorway.

"Hi, baby," she said, walking over to take a seat next to them.

"We were trying to be quiet. You needed some rest." Justin's big eyes looked up earnestly at his mother. If only Justin hadn't been so sweet, trying to let her sleep yesterday morning, none of this would have happened. No, Diana amended to herself. This wasn't Justin's fault. It was hers.

"Thank you," Diana said. Her eyes filled with tears even though her body was cried out.

"The boys want to go to school today," Aaron said. "I'm going to take them, and then we can go to the hospital together when I get back."

Diana nodded. He wasn't exactly demonstrating the same level of compassion and love that he'd shown her the previous afternoon, but he was there. He was taking care of things, and Diana would accept any small kindness that she could. She smiled at him, and when he returned it, her anxiety melted away. She knew that smile.

He said, "Try icing your face for a while. It might help with the swelling."

She hadn't paid any attention to the throbbing in her head until Aaron said those words. Now it was as if she could feel her own body again. She touched her chin, swollen and scabby from its collision with the ground; her forehead, protruding and oddly squishy, something like a water balloon.

As she ran water for a shower, Diana stared at herself in the mirror. She looked like a battered wife; that was her first thought. Then she thought, No—I look like a soldier. Someone who's been through a war. She hated both comparisons. But any analogy, however horrible, however trite, was better than the truth: she was a mother who was beaten by her twelve-year-old autistic son. She tried to make this fit within her previously held identity but fell short.

...

Walking into the hospital later that day, Diana's body was tight with worry. She grabbed Aaron's hand. She wasn't sure she'd be able to stomach what Dr. Jefferson had to say. More bad news? Would they send Max home for a repeat performance until they had to admit him to this hospital again? She hadn't been able to anticipate anything that had happened, and the thought of facing another hurdle filled her with despair. She followed Aaron into the elevator.

"I'm so sorry," she whispered, biting her lip.

"Hey." Aaron turned to Diana, looking into her green eyes. "Listen. I've had some time away, and I've given this whole thing some thought. We're both doing the best we can. It's terrible that Max is here. It's terrible that he acted the way he did. But I've decided to accept what the experts say. I've been an ass about the medication thing, and I'm sorry for putting you under even more stress." Aaron's eyes glistened, and Diana knew that he meant it. He looked down. "I meant to tell you all this under better circumstances, but you were so tired, and then . . ." He motioned to their surroundings, squeezing her hand.

Unable to speak, Diana wrapped her arms tightly around Aaron. She had promised herself that she wouldn't cry today, and if she opened her mouth, it would all be over.

The elevator dinged, indicating that they'd reached the fourth floor. A receptionist greeted them, took their information, and soon led them back to Dr. Jefferson's office. He looked up from his desk as they walked inside.

"Please, have a seat," Dr. Jefferson said, smiling.

Aaron and Diana took the two black plastic chairs on the opposite side of Dr. Jefferson's desk.

Dr. Jefferson introduced himself to Aaron and continued, "I'm the child and adolescent psychiatrist responsible for Max's care during his stay here. He's been evaluated by one of our psychologists and has an entire team of professionals looking after him. As protocol during mandatory hospitalizations, the hospital works with the county, so Max also has an assigned caseworker. Her name is Charlotte Johnston, and she's wonderful. She's worked with parents I've also worked with before. She'd like to meet with you today." Dr. Jefferson slid a folder across to Aaron and Diana. Inside was information about the services the county would provide their family, as well as a business card for Charlotte Johnston.

Aaron nodded. He was more interested in the present than the future.

"As for Max's case"—Dr. Jefferson cleared his throat—"there is a high degree of uncertainty about his response to psychotropic medication because of his fairly complex diagnostic presentation. Our psychologist was able to spend some time with him yesterday evening and, after observation and reviewing his history, has confirmed that Max is on the autism spectrum. However, he also seems to have mood disorder NOS, intermittent explosive disorder, and ADHD."

Diana stared at Dr. Jefferson for so long that he sniffed and discreetly checked his nose. The only word that came to her mind was *why?* Why did her son have to be burdened with such challenges? What had he, or any of them, done to deserve such brutal obstacles to living a normal life, whatever "normal" meant? As quickly as the thoughts consumed Diana, she tried to dismiss them. This wasn't about fairness. They weren't being punished. It just *was*, and as Max's parents, she and Aaron just had to keep trying their best for him.

"Go on," Diana said, looking at Aaron, who nodded.

"After talking with him and reviewing Max's charts, my recommendation is that we undergo a complete medication wash. We'll taper all of his medications so that we're dealing with *Max*, and not interaction effects."

Diana nodded. The new diagnoses were a lot to take in, but she felt a peace in her spirit now that someone had taken it out of her hands. Her relief, though, came with a degree of dread. Was this just the next hopeful stop on a journey that would never arrive where she wanted it to?

"Okay, Dr. Jefferson. What do we need to do?" Aaron asked, leaning forward.

"If you agree, we need to do a formal admission, and Max will be here between three and four weeks. Your insurance coverage should be good, but you'll need to contact them as well. We also need you to meet with Charlotte to make plans for his release. She'll call you once he's been formally admitted. When he is discharged, you will also receive a discharge plan with recommendations."

"We can do that," Aaron said, grateful for the action-able items.

"Can we see him?" Diana asked.

"You can. And I'm sure he'd like to see you." The only indication of Dr. Jefferson's smile was the curving of his thick beard around the corners of his mouth.

Aaron and Diana walked slowly across the white tile to the elevator, arm in arm. Aaron looked straight ahead, shell-shocked from his abrupt trip home and all the infor-mation that he'd received in the past twenty-four hours. Diana kept stride with him, and when they reached the elevator, Aaron pressed the button for the second floor.

"Three to four weeks here," Aaron finally said, break-ing the silence.

Diana sighed, staring at their distorted reflections in the closed elevator doors. "I know."

They waited for the elevator to arrive, lost in their own thoughts, memories, and worries. Finally, Diana said, "Whatever happens, we need to be partners in this, Aaron. We both love Max and want the best for him, but pulling in different directions will only tear us apart. I'm sorry," she said, looking down, "that I continued giving him medication when you were so obviously against it."

Aaron shifted so that he could wrap his arm around Diana's shoulders. "I didn't give you much choice, did I?"

The elevator dinged, and they stepped inside. Diana was grateful that it was empty. She looked into her husband's eyes, more deeply than she had in months, it seemed. He looked back at her. It was intimate and frightening and wonderful, this level of seeing each other.

"Partners?" she asked.

"Deal." Aaron kissed the top of her head. He hadn't

said that in years, but looking into Diana's eyes, he saw the flicker of recognition. When he'd been on one knee, fifteen years earlier, he'd worked hard to pour out his feelings, all of the promises he intended to keep with Diana for eternity. When he'd finished, he'd forgotten to ask whether she'd marry him, so his monologue ended with, "I want to keep you, forever." And she'd responded, "Deal." Left hand extended, she'd waited, smiling, for him to slip the ring on her finger. For years, the word had been a catch-all for them, but it had long since been relegated to the idealism of their youth. Hearing it again here, now, was incongruous and comforting at once.

CHAPTER 5

Diana had been nervous to speak with Charlotte Johnston. Aaron had spoken to her once before, six months earlier, when Max was hospitalized the first time. Aaron had re-assured her after the hospitalization that they were placing him in a therapeutic residential program and that they expected to see significant improvements. Diana's stomach had knotted when she considered having to tell the social worker that their plan had failed, and that they now needed the services they'd declined before. But Charlotte, when she'd called, had been warm and professional, not at all judgmental. Immediately, Diana had felt the tightness in her chest release. Charlotte would be an ally, she felt.

Now, two weeks after Max had been formally admitted, Charlotte's name appeared on Diana's phone. Diana had been expecting her call. Though Max would be in the hospital another two weeks, it was time to start talking about his release.

"Hi, Charlotte," Diana answered. She was just leaving the house to pick up the other boys from school, and momentarily the rumble of the garage door muted Charlotte's voice. "Sorry about that," Diana said, backing her car out.

"No worries," Charlotte replied. "How are you doing?"

"Well," Diana started. She wasn't used to answering that question, so she had no prepared response. "I'm okay," she said lamely. "Max seems to be doing better, but we sort of feel in limbo. We can't get used to a routine while he's gone, and I think all our nerves are on edge wondering how things will be when he's back home."

"Mmm," Charlotte said. "I can imagine how . . . precarious that must feel. Hopefully, though, we can start to shed a little light on things today. I'd like to talk to you about continued care and services for Max after he gets home."

The sky was heavy and white with clouds—a blank slate, Diana couldn't help thinking. That was the thing with being a mother: hope for her child's future did spring eternal, despite every previous disappointment.

"Please," Diana said, "tell me more."

"Well, I've talked with my supervisor, and even though Max is still on the waiting list for waiver services, they are willing to give your family an emergency slot. What this means is that Max qualifies for additional funding to support him in the home. You would begin to receive what is called ongoing services, which are services that are provided to children over the age of eight. We work really closely with an agency that provides community-based programming, and I'm hopeful they can help meet your family's needs."

Diana was nodding as Charlotte spoke. "That sounds fantastic," she said. "What do we have to do to get started?"

"I'd like to get the preliminary process going and refer you to a program that will provide ongoing services and continued therapy and care for Max when he gets back home," Charlotte replied. "The program that I'm talking about will ensure that he's receiving consistent thera-peutic support by working with you and your husband, your other sons, and with Max individually. They'll also consult and collaborate with the school, Max's psychia-trist, and other providers. The goal is to get everyone on the same page in order for Max to have the best possible care for his needs at home."

Diana was astounded. They were supposed to be on the waitlist for another *year*. "Charlotte, thank you. I don't know what to say."

Charlotte's voice was warm with a smile. "Say you'll sign the release of information form, which means you give me permission to forward all of Max's medical re-cords and reports to the program. We want them to come to you with a good idea of how to treat him and what you can expect."

"Absolutely," Diana said. "Just send me what I need to sign and I'll get it right over."

They talked for a few more minutes, with Charlotte telling Diana more about the assessment, which would be the next step after they received the release of infor-mation form. A clinical supervisor, who was a licensed psychologist, and a masters-level program coordinator would come to the house and talk to the family about their needs. For some, aggressive behavior, such as kick-ing, hitting, biting, and spitting, was the primary con-cern. Other children struggled with things like bedroom routine, personal hygiene, or daily living skills. Some parents just needed a break, a slice of two or three hours in which they could sleep or grocery shop or attend support meetings, all with the unimaginable ease of not having their special needs child with them. To Diana, the program sounded like a rescue. "It takes a village to raise a child" was the saying; it was probably coined by a parent of a child with autism, Diana thought dryly.

There had been a time, soon after Max was diagnosed, that Diana might have resisted such a service. She felt a deep sense of shame around Max's disorder, as if she had done something—when he was inside her, before he was conceived, after he screamed his way into the world—to cause it. Until he was eighteen months, he was developing normally. He was an easy baby, falling asleep quietly and completely, babbling sweetly in his stroller. She'd smile when exhausted friends told her how lucky she was that he slept through the night, that he didn't wail and scream. She'd nod, trying not to seem smug. And then, at that eighteen-month mark, something changed. It was as though a switch—so hidden they had yet to find it—had nudged itself off inside Max, and his deep blue eyes no longer recognized her. He stared past her or through her, avoiding her increasingly desperate gaze as she held him in her arms. She loved her son more than she ever thought possible—but she'd lost him, too. With Max, her heart was always split between grief and love, and in those early days, she couldn't bear for anyone to see it.

Now, though, she was like a misanthrope who'd realized she was the last person in the world—what she'd once eschewed, she now yearned for. Diana yearned for help. There was no pride or shame deep enough for her and Aaron to keep doing this by themselves.

...

Diana received a phone call from the program coordinator, Christine, the next afternoon, and they set up an appointment for the following week. Christine and a psychologist, Dr. Forde, arrived right on time. Christine wore a stylish pixie cut that showed off her vivid hazel eyes, but her attire was simple in dark jeans and a crewneck sweater. Dr. Forde was likely in her fifties, with pronounced laugh lines and, endearingly, clear braces on her bottom teeth.

"I'm so glad that we were able to meet with you so quickly," Christine said, following Diana toward the living room. "I know Max is coming home soon—how is your family feeling about that?"

Diana was slightly taken aback at Christine's direct, though friendly, question. They don't waste any time, she thought, and she was glad.

Diana wasn't sure how to answer. The Dutiful Mom wanted to paste on a smile and chirp, We're so excited to have him back! But she feared her voice would go shrill, and her freckles would burn under the scrutiny of two women who surely knew better than to believe such sweet simplicity.

"We're . . . anxious," Diana said instead, taking a seat on the floral love seat she'd inherited from her mother. "We all miss him, but at the same time, I think we're all a bit haunted by memories of the last incident. You read about that, I'm sure?"

Dr. Forde nodded. "It sounds like that was a scary day for your family—especially for Justin."

Unexpectedly, a lump rose to Diana's throat. She nodded. "How do you get over your brother choking you like that?" she asked. "We don't want him to be afraid of Max, but it's not as if we can promise something like that won't happen again. So how do we keep our children safe without reinforcing that there's something to fear?"

The garage door rumbled, and Diana was both re-lieved and disappointed by the interruption.

"That's my husband," she said. "He rescheduled his one o'clock appointment so he'd have some time with us."

Christine and Dr. Forde exchanged glances and nod-ded. Christine said, "That's great. We can't tell you the difference it makes to have both parents present and active participants in the treatment plan."

"Oh, Aaron's always been very involved," Diana said, hearing the pride in her voice despite just recently re-senting that involvement.

The back door opened and shut with characteristic loudness, and Aaron joined them in the living room. After introducing himself, he asked whether anyone wanted water or tea, and Diana mentally chastised her-self: he'd always been a better host than she.

Over the next half hour, Dr. Forde asked about Max's behaviors, as well as other services the family had re-ceived. Trying not to speak over each other, Diana and Aaron told them about the natural approach they'd taken for so long, about the speech and occupational therapy. They talked about the difficulties they'd had with medi-cations and Max's self-injurious behavior. They answered Dr. Forde's questions about "antecedents" to Max's melt-downs, and Diana realized that she still didn't know what had happened that morning Max had attacked Justin. A part of her hadn't thought it mattered; it could be anything, after all. But Dr. Forde encouraged her to ask the boys about it, because the more they could iden-tify those antecedents, the more they could begin to intervene before Max escalated. After their assessment,

Dr. Forde said, "I think your family would benefit from counseling and therapeutic services, along with daily living skills and respite. All of that combined should be a great combination for you."

Diana nodded eagerly. "Yes!" she said. "And that social skills group you mentioned," she said to Christine, referring to an earlier topic of conversation. "I think that sounds fantastic, too, but I think it might be wise to let Max get adjusted first."

Christine smiled. "Of course. The last thing I wanted to run by you—how do you feel about starting services prior to Max's return home? To get things ready?"

Diana looked at Aaron in surprise. "That's an option?" she asked.

"Well, the waiver won't cover it," Christine said, "but the county might. We'll make a recommendation in our treatment plan and go from there."

"Max has more than likely had a pretty rigid routine over the last few weeks," said Dr. Forde. "He's probably waking up and eating breakfast at the same time each day, for example, so he knows what to expect. That's a comfort for kiddos like Max. We know that's harder to achieve at home, especially with multiple children, so that's one area we'd like to target."

Christine nodded. "And it's just as important to work with you two and Max's brothers on the adjustment to having him home. How are the boys going to react to him after the last incident? As you said, Diana, we don't want to reinforce fear. We want to teach coping skills—how are they going to handle it when they're playing a game with Max and he gets mad that he loses and starts yelling or banging on things?"

Diana knew it was a rhetorical question, but she still wished she had an answer. "That all sounds great," she said finally. "I think that's exactly what we need."

Aaron nodded. "I can't tell you how relieved I feel to hear things like 'coping skills.' Ever since Max was diagnosed, we've been trying to fix him from the inside." He paused, backtracking. "Fixed isn't the right word. You know what I mean—anyway, it just seems obvious now that we need to approach this from both ends. Maybe we've done the boys a disservice," he said, looking at Diana, "somehow thinking they're not capable of learning"—he faltered, searching for words—"*behavioral strategies*."

"I just don't think we knew how to go about it," Diana said. "We still wouldn't, on our own."

Christine and Dr. Forde listened to the exchange quietly.

"It might not feel like it," Dr. Forde said, "but just this— the dialogue you two are having—is a great start."

Shyly almost, Diana reached for Aaron's hand. He took it, but his eyes were fixed straight ahead at the fireplace mantel, where Max, sitting slightly away from the family, stared from a framed photograph.

...

Shortly after their visit, Christine and Dr. Forde submitted their treatment plan to Charlotte, who approved the hours that were recommended. Charlotte also agreed to pay for five hours of in-home support per week prior to Max returning home. Plus, the occupational therapy Max received at school would increase due to his revised individualized education plan, or IEP. Max would also continue seeing Dr. Jefferson at his private practice for ongoing medication consultation.

Over the next two weeks, Aaron and Diana worked with Addyson, the lead clinical coordinator assigned to Max's case, and the behavior support specialists to ready themselves for Max's arrival. They'd prepared a daily and weekly visual schedule for Max's days at home, which they hung in various locations: on the fridge, in Max's bedroom, on the living room wall. Aaron and Diana had also participated in group therapy with their younger children to discuss the impact that Max's behavior had on family dynamics. They'd also finally talked about that morning.

"It's my fault," Justin said, ducking his head. "Mom was sleeping, so I went to make Max toast and I dropped the peanut butter knife and it clattered on the ground. Max started to get mad, but I was so tired, and I told him—" He looked up at Diana and Aaron, who both nodded encouragingly. "I told him to shut up. I said it kind of mean and kind of loud, like, 'Shut *up*, Max!' IwasjustsotiredandiwasmadbecauseMaxalwaysgetswhateverhewantsandwealljusthavetodealwithit." The words spilled from Justin in a breathless stream. His ears were red, and he could hardly look at the adults. "I'm sorry. It was all my fault."

Aiden watched the scene with his mouth slightly open, as if he couldn't believe Justin had confessed. He looked between the adults with a childish mixture of dread and delight.

"Oh, honey," Diana said, going to Justin. She squeezed beside him on the leather armchair and pulled him close. "No one blames you. We all get upset sometimes."

As she held him, she realized how little she'd considered what must be complex emotions for Justin. He was her shining optimist, the sweet spirit who'd told her to nap that morning, that he'd "make cereal." His eagerness to please had made him easy to overlook, in a way—easy to assume he was fine, healthy, happy. But how could he be if none of them were?

Addyson and the behavior support specialists worked to help the family better understand Max's deficits, reminding them that he might just need time to process what they told him. Aaron and Diana would begin with behavior modification services, which would focus on the specific behaviors they wanted to decrease, as well as teach them how to handle Max in certain situations. After that, the team would start to work specifically with Max on daily living skills. And hopefully soon, Addyson had told them, Diana and Aaron would be able to get some respite services so they could have a date night. The two had looked at each other and laughed, partly with humor, partly with sadness; neither could remember the last time they'd done something as a couple, and neither could quite be convinced that day would come any time soon.

...

"Okay, so remember what we've talked about." Addyson was sitting at the kitchen table with Aaron, Diana, and the boys. Max was coming home from the hospital that afternoon, and while anxiety was high, so was the family's excitement. "Our first goal is to provide Max with some realistic expectations, routine, structure, and predictability."

"Yes, ma'am!" Aiden said, saluting and clapping his heels together.

He was a little comedian, they'd realized in the last month. An inevitable class clown. "We're going to have to keep an eye on that one," Aaron had told Diana one night in bed. "He's gonna give us trouble one day." Diana had laughed. "I think we can handle it," she'd said.

"You're going to have to go soon," Addyson said, looking at her watch. "Do you have any questions for me before I head out?"

Aaron and Diana looked at each other. Diana took a deep breath and exhaled, feeling her anxiety. "I don't think so," she said. "For now, we're as ready as can be."

"Remember to follow the schedule consistently. Take notes on any triggers that precede behavioral problems, like anger and aggression, and also record how you respond so we can get a behavioral pattern of antecedents and consequences. I'll be back tomorrow to visit with you and meet Max, finally!" Addyson smiled, her cinnamon skin lighting up as she prepared to part ways for the day.

"Thank you," Diana said. "You've given us some great ideas."

Addyson waved to the boys before she walked to the front door. Suddenly, the house was silent.

Adrenaline and nerves pumped through them all, causing a throb that Diana could feel behind her eyes. She couldn't wait to have her little boy back. She might feel differently later—she almost certainly would, at some point—but for this moment, she ached for her firstborn, the first and truest experience she'd ever had of unconditional love.

Without a word, the family loaded into their car and drove to the hospital. In trying to keep Max to the schedule he'd grown accustomed to, they were picking him up after lunch, when he normally had free time with his peers in the game room.

They walked as a group into Max's hospital room to find him in his favorite green hoodie, sitting on the edge of his bed with his gaming device. He looked up and gave them a half smile before returning his attention to the game.

Aiden and Justin surrounded their brother, looking at the little screen and commenting on the game. Max laughed as Aiden pretended to shoot the bad guys with a pantomime gun. After a moment, he set down his game and without looking at him, stretched an arm toward Justin. Justin tensed and cast a quick, panicked look at Diana, but when he realized it was an embrace, he relaxed and leaned into Max's shoulder.

"Are you ready to go home, Max?" Diana asked, tears in her eyes as she watched her boys interact just like brothers.

"Game over," Max said, putting his game into the carrying case and standing to join his family.

CHAPTER 6

At first, when Charlotte Johnston had initially told Diana about ongoing services, five hours a week of support had seemed monumental—after all, it was five more hours than they'd ever had. Then, when Max returned and Addyson and her team began working with him, five hours seemed like not nearly enough. What could really be accomplished in only five hours a week? Diana had brought this up with Addyson, who had patted Diana's shoulder and said, "It's like therapy: you get out of it what you put in. If you leave after one hour and go back to your normal habits and behaviors, nothing changes. But if you take what you learned in that hour and apply it as intentionally and as often as you can, your whole life can change."

"In other words," Diana said back wryly, "stop whining and do the work."

Addyson laughed. "You said it."

While it was tempting to use the time Addyson was over to go to the office or attend to chores around the house, Diana participated in almost every session. Aaron's work schedule was less flexible, but he and Diana made time at least once a week to sit together and discuss the week's progress. And because it was summer, Justin and Aiden were a part of most sessions as well. Addyson explained to Diana that it was important for the rebuilding of their relationship that they do activities and play games together. They took turns blowing bubbles, or sat at the kitchen table with jars of finger paint and swiped vibrant lines of blue and green across craft paper. The activities were simple, but each one enforced care and collaboration, and demonstrated that Max wasn't only and always aggressive and destructive. He was also silly and focused and methodical. He was multidimensional, capable of pleasant surprises.

Of course, despite the behavioral improvements and the success with the medication and dosage Dr. Jefferson had prescribed, Max still struggled with change and transition, and with expressing his emotions before they escalated. Addyson had taught Diana and the boys to cue in to the early indications that Max was upset: he might flap his hands lightly in his lap or turn his head from side to side. They were small motions, innocuous and easy to miss. But when the family paid attention, they could ask him, "How are you feeling right now, Max?" and show him his picture book of emotions—cartoon faces ranging from joyful smiles to wide, surprised eyes to tearful to red faced. Max would point, and even if they didn't quite know *why* he was mad, they could intervene. They could say, "Let's go to your sensory box," and lead him to the small chest containing squeeze balls and his skin brusher and a weighted vest and a bubble gun. Max would pick what he needed, and they could say, "Do you want to go to your room for five minutes?" And Max could help them help him. Diana often wondered whether he felt more empowered, but of course, that was not a cartoon face he could point to.

One afternoon, Addyson asked Max, Diana, Justin, and Aiden to draw a picture of their fantasy island. "If you could take three things with you—anything you want—to your island, what would they be?"

The four of them sat on pillows around the living room coffee table, and for ten minutes, the room was silent save for the scratching of colored pencils on construction paper and their occasional contemplative sighs. Addyson waited until everyone had finished before asking, "Who wants to share first?"

Aiden's hand darted up. He stood and, holding the paper by the top corners like a matador's cape, twirled to show everyone. "Well, I drew my family," he said first, offhandedly, "but *then* I drew a river of chocolate! And a TV."

"Hey!" Justin said. "You copier! I drew my family, too. See, there's Mom and Dad, and there's Aiden, swinging from a tree like a monkey, and there's Max, playing with his game. I also put the whole Harry Potter series—because it's still just one thing," he said reasonably to Addyson, "and also a *dog*, because that would be *cool!*"

"A dog?" Diana laughed. "I didn't know you wanted a dog."

Justin looked at her incredulously. "Well, *yeah*," he said.

"Ooh, can we get a dog?" Aiden chimed in, jumping up and down. Quickly, he stopped himself. "Sorry, Max," he said, dropping back onto the pillow. "It's your turn."

Max shoved his paper toward Diana. In straight, strong lines, he'd drawn his game device, a swing, and two circles connected by an arch that Diana thought might be his headphones. It hadn't even occurred to Max to include his family. Diana registered this with deep but unsurprised sadness. That's okay, she thought at her unreachable angel. You just keep doing your best, and I'll keep doing mine, and we'll be okay.

The garage door rumbled open, and all three boys hopped to their feet. "Dad," Max said. To anyone else, the word would sound flat and unexcited, but Diana saw that Max was rubbing his thumb and middle finger together, the way he did before a favorite meal or blowing bubbles, and she thought, Drawing be damned—he loves us the way he knows how.

Addyson smiled and said, "We have just enough time for Dad to draw something, too."

"You heard her," Diana said. "Go get him!"

She smiled as the boys ran from the room, and then she traced her fingers over Max's drawing again. She couldn't help wondering what their lives would be like when Max was fifteen, twenty, forty . . . The thought, never far from her mind, was overwhelming in its uncertainty. But for now, they were here, they were together, and they were safe. Diana's prayers of a few months ago had been answered in Dr. Jefferson and Addyson and an entire support team; she had to believe that her prayers for the future would not go unheard, either.

HOW THESE BOOKS WERE CREATED

The ORP Library of disabilities books is the result of heartfelt collaboration between numerous people: the staff of ORP, including the CEO, executive director, psychologists, clinical coordinators, teachers, and more; the families of children with disabilities served by ORP, including some of the children themselves; and the Round Table Companies (RTC) storytelling team. To create these books, RTC conducted dozens of intensive, intimate interviews over a period of months and performed independent research in order to truthfully and accurately depict the lives of these families. We are grateful to all those who donated their time in support of this message, generously sharing their experience, wisdom, and—most importantly—their stories so that the books will ring true. While each story is fictional and not based on any one family or child, we could not have envisioned the world through their eyes without the access we were so lovingly given. It is our hope that in reading this uniquely personal book, you felt the spirit of everyone who contributed to its creation.

ACKNOWLEDGMENTS

Writing this book would not have been possible without the wisdom, patience, and experience of many generous individuals. In particular, the authors would like to thank retired Genesee Lake School health services director Karen Johnson and Genesee Lake School therapist Christy Lynch for providing valuable information and perspective on the realities and use of psychotropic medication with children. We would also like to thank Debbie Frisk, vice president of Oconomowoc Residential Programs, for her insights into day treatment programs, and Lorri Nelson, ORP executive assistant, for facilitating interviews, organizing material, and generally helping to wrangle the many moving parts that go into writing a book. Finally, we extend a heartfelt thank you to E. L. Mendoza and the other families who shared their journeys with autism spectrum disorder and psychotropic medications in such detail. This group of people was invaluable in bringing Max's story to life, and the authors are deeply grateful.

JEFFREY D. KRUKAR, PH.D.

BIOGRAPHY

Jeffrey Krukar, Ph.D., is a licensed psychologist and certified school psychologist with more than 20 years of experience working with children and families in a variety of settings, including community-based group homes, vocational rehabilitation services, residential treatment, juvenile corrections, public schools, and private practice. He earned his Ph.D. in educational psychology, with a school psychology specialization and psychology minor, from the University of Wisconsin-Milwaukee. Dr. Krukar is a Think:Kids Certified Trainer in Collaborative Problem Solving, and an assistant professor at the Wisconsin School of Professional Psychology. He is a registrant of the National Register of Health Service Providers in Psychology, and is also a member of the American Psychological Association.

As the psychologist at Genesee Lake School in Oconomowoc, WI, Dr. Krukar believes it truly takes a village to raise a child—to strengthen developmental foundations in relating, communicating, and thinking—so they can successfully return to their families and communities. Dr. Krukar hopes the ORP Library of disabilities books will bring to light the stories of children and families to a world that is generally not aware of their challenges and successes, as well as offer a sense of hope to those currently on this journey.

KATIE GUTIERREZ

BIOGRAPHY

Katie Gutierrez believes that a well-told story can tran-
scend what a reader "knows" to be real about the world—
and thus change the world for that reader. In every form,
story is transformative, and Katie is proud to spend her
days immersed in it as executive editor for Round Table
Companies, Inc.

Since 2007, Katie has edited approximately 50 books
and co-written several of the ORP Library of disabilities
books, including *Meltdown* and *An Unlikely Trust*. She has
been humbled by the stories she has heard and hopes
these books will help guide families on their often-lonely
journeys, connecting them with resources and support.
She also hopes they will give the general population a
glimpse into the Herculean jobs taken on so fiercely by
parents, doctors, therapists, educators, and others who
live with, work with, and love children like Max.

Katie holds a BA in English and philosophy from South-
western University and an MFA in fiction from Texas
State University. She has contributed to or been profiled
in publications including *Forbes*, *Entrepreneur* magazine,
People magazine, *Hispanic Executive Quarterly*, and *Narra-
tive* magazine. She can't believe she's lucky enough to do
what she loves every day.

CHELSEA McCUTCHIN

BIOGRAPHY

Chelsea McCutchin is a writer, student, teacher, daughter, wife, and mom. When she isn't doing all of the above, you can find her sleeping. Or dreaming. Sometimes at the same time.

NICOLETTE E. WEISENSEL, M.D., F.A.P.A.

BIOGRAPHY

Nicolette E. Weisensel, M.D., F.A.P.A., is a board-certified psychiatrist who has experience in a variety of practice settings including outpatient, inpatient, residential, and day treatment. She has expertise in the treatment of eating disorders and Prader-Willi syndrome. Dr. Weisensel earned her M.D. from the University of Wisconsin School of Medicine and Public Health. She also completed her psychiatry residency at the University of Wisconsin, serving as chief resident during her final year. She has presented at regional, national, and international conferences regarding eating disorders and Prader-Willi syndrome. She is a member and fellow of the American Psychiatric Association.

JAMES G. BALESTRIERI

BIOGRAPHY

James G. Balestrieri is currently the CEO of Oconomowoc Residential Programs, Inc. (ORP). He has worked in the human services field for over 40 years, holding positions that run the gamut to include assistant maintenance, assistant cook, direct care worker, teacher's aide, summer camp counselor, bookkeeper, business administrator, marketing director, CFO, and CEO. Jim graduated from Marquette University with a B.S. in Business Administration (1977) and a Master's in Business Administration with an emphasis in Marketing (1988). He is also a Certified Public Accountant (Wisconsin—1982). Jim has a passion for creatively addressing the needs of those with impairments by managing the inherent stress among funding, programming, and profitability. He believes that those with a disability enjoy rights and protections that were created by the hard-fought efforts of those who came before them; that the Civil Rights movement is not just for minority groups; and that people with disabilities have a right to find their place in the world and to achieve their maximum potential as individuals. For more information, see *www.orp.com*.

ABOUT ORP

Oconomowoc Residential Programs, Inc. is an employee-owned family of companies making a difference in the lives of people with disabilities. With service locations throughout Wisconsin and Indiana, our dedicated staff of 2,400 people provides quality services and professional care to more than 1,950 children, adolescents, and adults with special needs. ORP provides a comprehensive continuum of care. Child and adolescent programs include developmentally appropriate education and treatment in settings specifically attuned to their needs. These include residential therapeutic education and vocational services for students from all around the country. For those in or near Wisconsin and Indiana, we offer community-based residential supports, in-home supports, in- and out-of-home respite care, and alternative therapeutic day school programs. We provide special programs for students with specific academic and social issues relative to a wide range of complex disabilities, including autism spectrum disorders, Asperger's disorder, cognitive and developmental disabilities, anxiety disorders, depression, bipolar disorder, reactive attachment disorder, attention deficit disorder, severe emotional and behavioral issues, Prader-Willi syndrome, and other impairments. Our adult services continuum includes community-based residential services for people with intellectual, developmental, and physical disabilities, brain injury, mental health and other behavioral impairments, and the medically fragile.

We also provide independent living homes, supervised apartments, community-based supports for adults in mental health crisis, day service programs, and respite services.

At ORP, our guiding principle is passion: a passion for the people we serve and for the work we do.

For a comprehensive look at each of our programs, please visit *www.orp.com*. For a collection of resources for parents, educators and administrators, and health-care professionals who are raising or supporting children with disabilities, please visit the ORP Library at *www.orplibrary.com*.

RESOURCES FOR FAMILIES, LOVED ONES, AND PROFESSIONALS

American Academy of Child and Adolescent Psychiatry
www.aacap.org

American Psychiatric Association
www.psychiatry.org

Mayo Clinic
www.mayoclinic.org

National Alliance on Mental Illness (NAMI)
www.nami.org

National Institute of Mental Health
www.nimh.nih.gov

Understanding Mental Disorders: Your Guide to DSM-5

University of Wisconsin Hospital and Clinics
www.uwhealth.org

PSYCHOTROPIC MEDICATIONS

Connecting with Max is the second of three books in the ORP Library focusing on the use of psychotropic medication in children and adolescents. Based on dozens of interviews with parents and clinicians, this book tells the fictional (but all too real) story of Max, a twelve-year-old diagnosed with autism spectrum disorder. The book follows *Finding Balance*, which tells the story of seventeen-year-old Alex, who has been diagnosed with bipolar disorder. From exploring challenges with side effects, treatment adherence, and dosage and medication changes, to highlighting successes and explaining the importance of a comprehensive biopsychosocial treatment plan, this book series aims to educate families, caregivers, and healthcare professionals on the short-term and long-term impact of including psychotropic medication in a child's treatment plan.

FINDING BALANCE

A FAMILY'S JOURNEY TO TREATMENT FOR BIPOLAR DISORDER

CONNECTING WITH MAX

HOW MEDICATION CLOSED THE GAP BETWEEN A FAMILY AND THEIR SON WITH AUTISM

Look for additional books on children and psychotropic medications coming soon!

ASPERGER'S DISORDER

Meltdown and its companion comic book, *Melting Down*, are both based on the fictional story of Benjamin, a boy diagnosed with Asperger's disorder and additional challenging behavior. From the time Benjamin is a toddler, he and his parents know he is different: he doesn't play with his sister, refuses to make eye contact, and doesn't communicate well with others. And his tantrums are not like normal tantrums; they're meltdowns that will eventually make regular schooling—and day-to-day life—impossible. Both the prose book, intended for parents, educators, and mental health professionals, and the comic for the kids themselves demonstrate that the journey toward hope isn't simple . . . but with the right tools and teammates, it's possible.

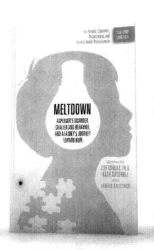

MELTDOWN

ASPERGER'S DISORDER,
CHALLENGING BEHAVIOR,
AND A FAMILY'S JOURNEY
TOWARD HOPE

MELTING DOWN

A COMIC FOR KIDS WITH
ASPERGER'S DISORDER AND
CHALLENGING BEHAVIOR

AUTISM SPECTRUM DISORDER

Mr. Incredible shares the fictional story of Adam, a boy diagnosed with autistic disorder. On Adam's first birthday, his mother recognizes that something is different about him: he recoils from the touch of his family, preferring to accept physical contact only in the cool water of the family's pool. As Adam grows older, he avoids eye contact, is largely nonverbal, and has very specific ways of getting through the day; when those habits are disrupted, intense meltdowns and self-harmful behavior follow. From seeking a diagnosis to advocating for special education services, from keeping Adam safe to discovering his strengths, his family becomes his biggest champion. The journey to realizing Adam's potential isn't easy, but with hope, love, and the right tools and teammates, they find that Adam truly is *Mr. Incredible*. The companion comic in this series, inspired by social stories, offers an innovative, dynamic way to guide children—and parents, educators, and caregivers—through some of the daily struggles experienced by those with autism.

MR. INCREDIBLE

A STORY ABOUT AUTISM,
OVERCOMING CHALLENGING
BEHAVIOR, AND A FAMILY'S FIGHT
FOR SPECIAL EDUCATION RIGHTS

INCREDIBLE ADAM
AND A DAY WITH AUTISM

AN ILLUSTRATED STORY
INSPIRED BY SOCIAL NARRATIVES

BULLYING

Nearly one third of all school children face physical, verbal, social, or cyber bullying on a regular basis. Educators and parents search for ways to end bullying, but as that behavior becomes more sophisticated, it's harder to recognize and stop. In *Classroom Heroes*, Jason is a quiet, socially awkward seventh grader who has long suffered bullying in silence. His parents notice him becoming angrier and more withdrawn, but they don't realize the scope of the problem until one bully takes it too far—and one teacher acts on her determination to stop it. Both *Classroom Heroes* and *How to Be a Hero*—along with a supporting coloring book (*Heroes in the Classroom*) and curriculum guide (*Those Who Bully and Those Who Are Bullied*)—recognize that stopping bullying requires a change in mindset: adults and children must create a community that simply does not tolerate bullying. These books provide practical yet very effective strategies to end bullying, one student at a time.

CLASSROOM HEROES

ONE CHILD'S STRUGGLE WITH BULLYING AND A TEACHER'S MISSION TO CHANGE SCHOOL CULTURE

HOW TO BE A HERO

A COMIC BOOK ABOUT BULLYING

HEROES IN THE CLASSROOM

AN ACTIVITY BOOK ABOUT BULLYING

THOSE WHO BULLY AND THOSE WHO ARE BULLLIED

A GUIDE FOR CREATING HEROES IN THE CLASSROOM

FAMILY SUPPORT

Schuyler Walker was just four years old when he was diagnosed with autism, bipolar disorder, and ADHD. In 2004, childhood mental illness was rarely talked about or understood. With knowledge and resources scarce, Schuyler's mom, Christine, navigated a lonely maze to determine what treatments, medications, and therapies could benefit her son. In the years since his diagnosis, Christine has often wished she had a "how to" guide that would provide the real mom-to-mom information she needed to survive the day and, in the end, help her family navigate the maze with knowledge, humor, grace, and love. Christine may not have had a manual at the beginning of her journey, but she hopes this book will serve as yours.

CHASING HOPE
YOUR COMPASS FOR A NEW NORMAL
NAVIGATING THE WORLD
OF THE SPECIAL NEEDS CHILD

PRADER-WILLI SYNDROME

Estimated to occur once in every 15,000 births, Prader-Willi syndrome is a rare genetic disorder that includes features of cognitive disabilities, problem behaviors, and, most pervasively, chronic hunger that leads to dangerous overeating and its life-threatening consequences. *Insatiable: A Prader-Willi Story* and its companion comic book, *Ultra-Violet: One Girl's Prader-Willi Story*, draw on dozens of intensive interviews to offer insight into the world of those struggling with Prader-Willi syndrome. Both books tell the fictional story of Violet, a vivacious young girl born with the disorder, and her family, who—with the help of experts—will not give up their quest to give her a healthy and happy life.

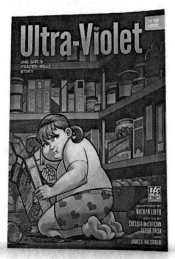

INSATIABLE
A PRADER-WILLI STORY

ULTRA-VIOLET
ONE GIRL'S PRADER-WILLI STORY

REACTIVE ATTACHMENT DISORDER

Loving Harder, *An Unlikely Trust*, and *Alina's Story* share the journeys of children diagnosed with reactive attachment disorder. *Loving Harder* is the true story of the Hetzel family, while *An Unlikely Trust* is a composite story based on dozens of intensive interviews with parents and clinicians. *Alina's Story* is a companion children's book and valuable therapeutic tool, offering a beautiful and accessible way for children with RAD to understand their own stories. The families in these books know their adopted children need help and work endlessly to find it, eventually discovering a special school that will teach the children new skills. Slowly, the children get better at expressing their feelings and solving problems. For the first time in their lives, they realize they are safe and loved . . . and capable of loving in return.

AN UNLIKELY TRUST

ALINA'S STORY OF ADOPTION,
COMPLEX TRAUMA,
HEALING, AND HOPE

ALINA'S STORY

LEARNING HOW
TO TRUST,
HEAL, AND HOPE

LOVING HARDER

OUR FAMILY'S ODYSSEY
THROUGH ADOPTION AND
REACTIVE ATTACHMENT
DISORDER

CPSIA information can be obtained at www.ICGtesting.com
Printed in the USA
LVOW10s0022260316

480793LV00001B/1/P